MOTHERHOOD AND FEMINISM

Motherhood and Feminism

Copyright © 2010 by Amber E. Kinser, PhD
Published by
Seal Press
A Member of the Perseus Books Group
1700 Fourth Street
Berkeley, California

Library of Congress Cataloging-in-Publication Data

Kinser, Amber E., 1963-
Motherhood and feminism / Amber E. Kinser.
p. cm.
Includes index.
ISBN 978-1-58005-270-2
1. Motherhood. 2. Feminism--History. I. Title.
HQ759.K552 2010
306.874'3--dc22
                2009049392

9 8 7 6 5 4 3 2 1

Cover design by Kate Basart, Union Pageworks
Cover illustration by Lauren Simkin Berke c/o rileyillustration.com
Book design by Mike Walters
Printed in the United States of America
Distributed by Publishers Group West

MOTHERHOOD AND FEMINISM

AMBER E. KINSER, PhD

SEAL
Studies

To my mother,
Gail Walters, whom I adore

CONTENTS

PROLOGUE

THE SEEDS OF FEMINIST MOTHERING were sown for me by my mother, who was not a feminist. By the time I really got into feminist writing and theory, which was also about the time I ventured into mothering, my thinking had already been cultivated by years of watching her live her life and raise her children in self-determined ways. In my memories she always worked outside the home as well as within it, though she tells me she withdrew from paid work at different times when each of her four children was very young to care for the new baby at home. As a member of the working class in the 1960s, she relied on a network of women neighbors and friends with whom she exchanged childcare. She had her own money and so was in a position to make most of the decisions about how we were raised—our clothing, our food, our school supplies, our health and dental care, our holiday gifts. On large purchases such as our home, furniture, transportation, school tuition, and vacations, she and my dad made decisions together, with her having significant influence on how things shook out for us. Even though she worked in paid employment, she considered herself a homemaker and put a great deal of time and energy into this part of her identity. To be able to bring in income and pull off the kind of mothering she had plotted out for herself, to do a shift at work and also cook, clean, make and launder our clothes, garden, can food, bathe and put us to bed, plus chaperone elementary school field trips and orchestrate family outings and celebrations, she had to pull a "second shift" at home at the end of every workday and continue to work like that all weekend long. She made strategic use of the children in these efforts, employing us in an expansive range of home care and food preparation activities. This helped to distribute the labor among more people but certainly saddled her with managing our work. My dad's days were shorter than my mom's, though he usually held two jobs and worked about two-thirds of his weekends. For the most part, when my dad was home, he was "off"; my mother led a very different life.

I always assumed I would have children, and I always assumed I would work. It never occurred to me to do things any other way. I do wonder what decisions I would have made if the choice not to have children had been presented to me as an option. The phrase "when you have children" prefaced many comments from my parents; "*if* you have children" never did. What also never occurred to me was how much of a struggle that managing motherhood and career would require. As an adult, I had to work, and still do, to plot out a self-determined, empowered motherhood for myself. In some ways this has not been so hard, because I learned so much from my mother about calling the shots in the affairs of the home and children, about working toward what I want out of life and being sure to earn my own money, and about my right to leave a marriage if I needed to. I also learned from her that kids don't need you to micromanage every aspect of their lives; they don't need to be in multiple after-school activities; they function fine without their mother at every field trip, track meet, or school day event; they don't have to be supervised all the time; and they can make their way back home safely.

But in other ways it has been difficult. Following my mother's example would mean that I would carry an unjust burden for home and family care and that I would forfeit, for a sizable part of my adult life, a college education and a career and the higher income and status that often go with them. It would mean that I'd have to convince myself that men are simply less capable of nurturing care than women, and I know this to be false. It would mean that at the end of every workday I'd have to put great stock in multidish family dinners, the planning and preparation for which I simply can't manage, don't care to manage, and frankly am not that good at. It would mean that I would begin figuring out who I am beyond my home and community only when my children were grown. But none of this speaks to who I am, so I've had to cut new paths for myself. I haven't always known how to do that and have often felt that I was making motherhood from scratch. But feminism taught me I had the right and the internal resources to construct a mother role and identity that were of my own design, even if they didn't follow cultural standards, and I had a right to the external resources that would help me do that. Feminism also taught me that I don't have to sacrifice what is right for me in order for my family to flourish. When my children were very young, I parented them with their dad; now I parent them with their stepdad, and their dad remains an important part of their lives. The dynamics of stepfamilies and coparenting make life pretty complicated at times, but our family structure has allowed all of us to prosper in our own ways.

I had my daughter and son when I was twenty-seven and thirty-three, respectively. My mother's open attitude and frank discussions about sex when I was young (which included taking me to the doctor to start me on the Pill when I was sixteen and sexually active) and later my access to birth control, the ability to (just barely) afford it, partners who took contraception seriously too, and the good luck that my birth control didn't fail meant that I had the two children I wanted at the times in my life when I was ready for them and when I felt I could best mother them. I raised them while working on my doctoral degree and beginning my career as a professor, so they've always known me to be involved in things that mattered to me but didn't have much to do with them. I imagine that they wish I could have been more available to them for their school and after-school activities than I was, but I also know that they both have learned from me that women are persons in their own right and are not solely defined by motherhood. This is a lesson about the personhood of women that they will take with them and use the rest of their lives. Teaching them this through example was not easy in a national workplace climate that ignores the fact that employees are usually attached to families, into which they pour a great deal of passion and energy. Universities, in particular, are teeming with activity in the evenings, activities that young professionals are expected to attend, and they load professors up with work that they often end up taking home. So I frequently felt pulled between my identity as a professor and my identity as a mother.

One evening I was a speaker on a panel that was discussing the presidential election; I was the only woman on the panel with four other speakers and a moderator. The discussion went on and on, and I wanted to get home to my children, whom I hadn't seen all day; I wanted to see them to bed and tell them good night. Neither the panelists nor the moderator seemed concerned about the time and whether people had time limitations and family commitments after the event; it seemed that none of them had either. The discussion continued and I was at a loss for how to handle the situation. Finally, when the discussion topic came around to me again, I said, "I'm going to make this one comment and then I've got to go home and tuck my children into bed," and I made my comment and left. By the time I got home, my children were drifting off, so I don't think I satisfied anybody that night. I have second-guessed myself many times as a mother and as a professional, and I have felt guilt ridden many others. The struggle for me has been to allow neither the people at work nor the people in my home to define me, but instead to define myself. That's a difficult distinction to make, however, because I have found so much of who I am in mothering and in teaching and writing.

I was pregnant with my oldest, my daughter, when I was working on my PhD and I started finding ways to make all my research papers be about pregnancy. This allowed me to immerse myself in feminist theory and produce the papers I was supposed to produce while still being very focused on my own experience. I have done this same kind of writing ever since. My dissertation was about how women experience and talk about pregnancy. My writing and research that followed was about raising a daughter as a feminist, and then about raising a son as a feminist. More recently I've written about mothering in the third wave of feminism, up against postfeminism, and amid the unrealistic expectations that characterize views of motherhood today. So for me, my creative and professional lives have always been interwoven with my family experience. In writing this book, I've learned that my interweaving of feminism and mothering has a long tradition. I learned from my foremothers—the feminist leaders, woman advocates, and moms before me—that public life and private life inform each other and conflict with each other. This book is about how mothers—past and present—have worked against the division of these two realms, to honor women as individuals and as parts of families and communities.

CHAPTER 1

AN OVERVIEW OF FEMINIST WRITING ON MOTHERHOOD

VOLUNTARY MOTHERHOOD, THE FEMININE MYSTIQUE, racial uplift, revalorist feminism, the mother heart, the second shift, othermothering, the new momism, the mommy wars—all of these phrases serve as cultural flashpoints that highlight the complex, dynamic, and sometimes contentious relationship between feminism and motherhood. Feminist writers and activists in the United States have moved at various points in history between celebrating motherhood, critiquing it, using it as leverage to gain other rights, and reconceptualizing it so that mothering can be a more empowering experience for women. Feminists have worked to honor mothering as a center of most women's lives, whether they have cared for their own or other children, and whether they have come to care for such children by birth, adoption, marriage or long-term commitment, community relationships, or other connections. Writers as diverse as literary novelists, feminist theorists, and bloggers in the online "mamasphere" have examined the ways in which the practices of mothering have shaped women's lives. They have articulated the complex tasks of caring for others and teaching children how to function effectively in their social worlds, a task typically performed by mothers and mother figures. Feminists have also channeled a great deal of energy into critiquing motherhood as a source of women's oppression, isolation in the home, and exclusion from paid work and career opportunities. These writers and thinkers have examined the ways that expectations for how women should mother are entwined with a host of other social expectations and often have little to do with

1

what is best for women or children. Rather, feminists have argued, expectations for "good" mothering are grounded in the interests of male dominance, capitalism, religious power, homophobia, and racism. In addition to honoring and critiquing motherhood, feminists have employed women's roles as mothers as a way to strengthen their arguments on other matters. From this perspective, feminists have asserted that a woman's obligations as a mother uniquely position her to comment on social problems and issues. Her "mother knowledge" about human needs and relationships and her ability to manage the details of multiple lives at once can be applied outside the immediate context of home and family and can inform and benefit other social arenas and concerns, such as politics, community relationships, peace, and environmental justice.

The relationship of feminism to motherhood has clearly been a complex one, even an ambivalent one. There has been no single, unified, monolithic response coming from feminism about motherhood, or about anything else for that matter. Feminists have always spoken from a variety of perspectives, from a range of beliefs, worldviews, and experiences. This many-sidedness, or polyvalence, in feminism is a sign of lively debate, intellectual rigor, and willingness to change. Feminists have addressed a broad range of issues related to motherhood, and they have done so by employing differing, and sometimes contradictory, arguments. Ideas of mothering and family have changed significantly through time in the broader culture as well. As you read about the diversity of thought in feminism and the ways that ideas about motherhood have been conceived differently by people through U.S. history, consider the ways that each of us can play a part in deciding how motherhood is defined and whether mothering functions as an empowering experience for women or an oppressive one.

Examining Power and Agency

Feminism in general is concerned with how power is constructed and divided in public and personal lives, and how women's lives are affected by that. It looks at how power is allocated in relationships, in the home, between social groups, and within institutions such as education, healthcare, government, the media, and the workplace. It has looked at the ways that gender, as well as race, sexuality, class, and ability, influence those allocations, though much of the published feminist work on power has focused predominately on how men are advantaged in social power at women's expense. Feminist attention to mothering examines how unequal allocations of power impinge upon women's experiences of parenting and impede their ability to adequately care for their children while living full and purposeful lives.

One principal goal of feminist analyses of power is to break down current power relations and rebuild them in more equitable ways. Feminists have argued for a change in the sexist status quo, which gives men and their lives greater authority, resources, and status. Women's lives and the activities in which they engage—such as mothering—are seen as less interesting, less important, and less worthy of economic, political, religious, and historical attention and support. Changing the status quo so that it distributes power more equitably would afford women more authority, better resources, and higher status. As a consequence, they would have greater agency—the ability to act in ways that are self-determined. In other words, they would be better able to act as the agents of their own needs and desires, including determining and meeting the needs of their children.

For a woman, being able to decide if and when she wants to become a mother is a critical starting place for her power. To exercise full agency in this way, a woman must have knowledge about reproductive processes, sexuality, contraception, adoption, abortion, and other variables so that she can make informed decisions. She also has to have the power to say when she would be sexually active and with whom. Much feminist effort has been channeled into ensuring that women have this knowledge and freedom to act on it in the best interests of their families and/or themselves. Feminists have also demonstrated the links between women's race, class, and other social factors and their ability to control their own reproduction. For example, historians such as Paula Giddings and Rickie Solinger documented how among enslaved women such agency was denied and yet sometimes practiced covertly. Most enslaved women in the southern United States were forced to bear numerous children to increase slaveholdings. Sometimes owners required the women to have multiple sex partners, and other times the owners themselves impregnated them, often through rape. But some physicians and slave owners complained that entire families or plantations of slave women would have no children for the master. Few of these women ever got pregnant, and when they did, they terminated their pregnancies; such practices were kept secret among the slave women. Women with knowledge of these secrets were able to actively resist efforts to control their reproduction and reclaim some measure of power in their lives.

A woman's ability to earn a wage is another important part of her ability to exercise power. Elizabeth Cady Stanton and other early feminists argued this in the "Declaration of Sentiments and Resolutions" at the first women's rights convention in Seneca Falls, New York, in 1848. Specifically, they argued that women were entitled to keep the wages they earned rather than relinquish them to their husbands. Fifty years later, author and humanist Charlotte Perkins Gilman wrote *Women and Economics*, in which she advocated for women's economic independence and proposed the idea of communal rearing of children to facilitate it—an idea that was already in practice among the working class and poor, as well as among Native and immigrant populations. The right of access to the workforce and a living wage continues to capture much feminist attention. As feminist maternal writer Andrea O'Reilly has pointed out in her recent book *Rocking the Cradle*, not only do economically empowered women have greater opportunity to live in more self-determined ways, but they also are able to be better champions for their children because they have the power to say how their children's material and educational needs will be met, and they have the financial resources to back it up.

Feminist scholar Sally Roesch Wagner points out in her book *Sisters in Spirit: Haudenosaunee (Iroquois) Influence on Early American Feminists* that the ideas of Stanton and her contemporaries about economic and social power in the family and the larger community were not new, or their own, but were instead pulled from the practices and belief systems of Haudenosaunee women, who already had a clear understanding of equal power distribution and why the family and larger community benefit from it. Native American scholar Barbara Alice Mann explains in her book *Iroquoian Women* that these Native communities had an even earlier and broader influence. Mann points out that early feminist writer Mary Wollstonecraft drew from Iroquoian women's beliefs and practices in writing her book *A Vindication of the Rights of Woman*; the book was published in 1792 and was distributed in Europe and the United States. Perhaps if feminism had observed and honored more keenly the social patterns and worldviews of these and other Native women, the United States would be much further along in its understanding and development of women's power more broadly.

Feminists have also worked to strengthen women's power by valuing and increasing their knowledge. One way they have done this is by rejecting popular beliefs that medical and psychological health professionals are the most reliable and important repositories of expertise about pregnancy, birth, and child rearing. Recognizing that knowledge is power, 21st-century writers, such as online "mommy bloggers" and other contributors to the mamasphere, have collaborated to develop countless resources for women that draw from the experiences of other mothers. Rather than draw only or primarily on the contributions of medical or psychology "experts," a wide range of women have used the Internet as an informative, motivating, and creative force for mothers and their children. May Friedman and Shana Calixte's book *Mothering and Blogging: The Radical Act of the MommyBlog* and Judith Stadtman Tucker's website The Mother's Movement Online are just two examples of work that explores how contemporary mothers have used technology to support and grow women's power in mothering knowledge. In this way, power is reconfigured so that mothers value their own and each other's mothering experiences and expertise.

A second principal goal in feminist analyses of power is to look at the multiple ways in which women exercise power *already*, despite the status quo, and examine more creatively how women explore and exercise agency. Rather than accept the proposition that women have no power and are only hapless victims, or that women's power needs to look like men's in order to count, feminists have observed the myriad ways that women determine the courses of their own lives. "Revalorist" feminists, for example, center their work on preserving women's traditional activities and advocating greater appreciation for what women have contributed within their traditional roles as mothers. Some revalorists identify as feminists but do not focus on equality between the sexes because they view "equality" to mean "sameness," an idea that conflicts with their view that women and men are inherently different. Other feminist revalorist work, such as that by Karen Foss and Sonja Foss, focuses on equality and women's traditional activity at the same time. In their book *Women Speak: The Eloquence of Women's Lives,* they show how the traditionally "feminine" activities of gardening, quilting, letter writing, and family storytelling have put women at the center of family, community cohesion, and relationship building. Through these activities, women play a highly influential role in shaping their own, their families', and their community members' lives and identities. They are therefore equally as powerful as men in shaping society and should be afforded equal social status and opportunity.

Historian Kim Anderson's work on Native women's mothering suggests that in indigenous cultures, women's traditional roles have long been recognized and celebrated as powerful, and they continue to be so today. Agency for Native women has emerged in part from the fact that even though social responsibilities are often divided along gender lines, masculine dominance is not a cultural value in their communities. These women do not view their work as having lower status. They also understand power to be grounded in women's ability to create and to nurture life. Because Native principles link women's creative power to that of the earth, mothers' efforts must be reciprocated, not simply taken from them. For a mother to continue providing, she must be mutually nourished and cared for, much as the earth must be cared for and replenished. From this belief system, Native mothers and the earth are to be both sources and recipients of care. The oppression of Native peoples makes this belief system difficult to fully realize. Relegation of Native communities to reservation life, which is marked by limited possibilities for earning decent wages and a restricted quality of life, and frequently by close proximity to environmentally unhealthy and even toxic areas, compounded by the lower social status ascribed to people of color and working-class or poor people, has resulted in reduced social power for Native women than was the case before contact with white culture. Nevertheless, many Native women find traditional female activities and belief in their natural power as childbearers to be powerful means of exercising agency.

While some feminists have looked at how motherhood functions as an oppressive aspect of women's lives, other feminists have looked at how it can be an important source of power for women. Some writers, particularly radical feminists in the 1960s and the early 1970s such as Shulamith Firestone and Ti-Grace Atkinson, indicated that joy in motherhood is a kind of "false consciousness," that it really is a powerless relation and that women are duped into thinking that it holds any promise of sovereignty or free expression. However, in the mid-1970s feminist writers Jessie Bernard and Adrienne Rich made important distinctions between the patriarchal institution of motherhood and women's actual experiences of mothering. Rich in particular argued that these experiences are not necessarily oppressive. Many feminists have argued since then that the degree of women's power in mothering, how it is lived out and experienced by the women themselves, and the social structures that encourage or discourage maternal agency are important points for consideration. This approach takes us beyond simple questions of whether mothers "have" agency or not and, understanding that they do, invites us to examine a more multilayered image of maternal power.

A majority of writers have not taken the position that being a mother is inherently oppressive, largely because it implies that mothers are completely powerless, which buttresses the patriarchal position that women's lives are little worth attending to. Further, this position

Mealtime Lessons from Mom

Sharon Goldberg is a mother who was born in the Midwest in 1940. In this passage from *Generations: A Century of Women Speak About Their Lives*, she reflects on her mother's life raising children in the 1940s and 1950s and how it affected her own rearing of three children.

My mother was a housewife and really loved taking care of the children. She made a very big business out of making three meals and cleaning. She had no other life. My mother was very bright. She loved books, but she was afraid to leave the confines of her kitchen. Women [like her] didn't work. My aunt, my mother's sister, went to law school and graduated and passed the bar. She never practiced.

We had this kitchen with a breakfast room off of it. And here we were, me, my three brothers, and my father. My father would be the first one to sit down and start eating. My mother would dish it all out, and everyone would start, and I would say, "Hey, did anyone think that maybe we could wait until Ma sits down?" and they'd say no, and they wouldn't. By the time she served everyone, they were finished, and my mother would eat afterwards, and I'd say, "What are you, the maid? Why do you do this? This is so awful." She'd say, "What's my choice? It needs to be hot." I said, "Serve it cold." She cared so much that it be hot and wonderful that it never dawned on her she was acting like a servant.

My father was the worst one—he'd say, "Ethel, I want my tea," and she'd get it. I'd say, "What are you doing getting him tea for? You eat, and then give him the tea." It was so horrible. I was so embarrassed for my mother. . . .

From the beginning when I had children, I would say, "Anybody picks up a fork before I sit down, I'm taking your food away."

also implies that nothing women have done has emerged from their own sense of self and agency, that everything about their actions and their lives has been determined for them. These implications are antithetical to feminism. They are also antithetical to positions taken by many women of color, both inside and outside of feminism. For instance, several Native women elders, such as Lena Sooktis (Northern

Cheyenne), Cecilia Mitchell (Akwesasne), and others featured in Steve Wall's *Wisdom's Daughters: Conversations with Women Elders of Native America*, argue strongly for embracing the links between women's childbearing function and their power in the community. Because the white majority has attempted to control the reproduction of African Americans, Native Americans, and immigrants through sterilization and other abuses, women in these communities often view pregnancy, childbearing, and mothering as a privilege rather than a trap.

Challenging Assumptions, Confronting Dualisms

A primary role of feminism throughout history has been to challenge taken-for-granted assumptions that direct our lives. This is difficult because people don't usually notice the assumptions that underpin our everyday lives. So challenging basic assumptions is often met with resistance, partly because it makes people uncomfortable. People often prefer to think that things just *are* the way they are and that nobody *made* them that way. So for example, it's easier for people to think that women just *are* more nurturing and that men just *are* more aggressive than it is to think that maybe we create the conditions that encourage men to be aggressive and discourage women from being that way or that we encourage women to be nurturing and discourage men from being that way. People also resist challenging assumptions when they see they have something to lose if they and others abandoned those assumptions. I think it would be difficult for my mother, for example, to believe that my father *could* have been more nurturing and less aggressive, partly because she would then have to make sense of living with his perpetual anger and his withdrawal from home care and childcare. I think it would be hard for my father to accept that my mother *works hard* at being nurturing and caring, rather than doing so as naturally and effortlessly as, say, breathing, because then he would have to make sense of why he left all of that hard work to her. Feminists have worked to challenge basic assumptions about whose needs "get to count" at home, at work, and in the bedroom; about what work "gets to count" as important enough to warrant respect, support, and fair compensation; about which version of what makes healthy, functional children "gets to count."

Confronting dualisms has been an important way to challenge taken-for-granted assumptions. Dualisms afford one social group higher status and more power than another. Dominant cultural assumptions that give men's lives primary importance are rooted in the practice of splitting concepts in two (creating a binary) and then heralding and celebrating one side of the binary while denigrating and disempowering the other (creating a hierarchy). Some general examples of gender-related dualisms include the conceptual splits between men as initiators of sex and women as receivers of sex, between the sperm as active and the egg as passive, and between men as aggressive and women as nurturing. Feminists have examined the problems of dualistic thinking and its impact on women's lives. Much of that critique is grounded in the argument that the problem lies first in the *split*, in the assumption that there are only two ways to consider a concept. A binary split of human phenomena not only oversimplifies the complexity of human societies and causes us to miss or ignore multiple possibilities for how we might think and live, but it also rather *invites* a hierarchical placing. This placing then results in arbitrary differences in power and agency among societal members. Part of feminist thinking, then, includes turning a critical eye toward binaries wherever they pop up, including in the realm of motherhood.

The split between the mind and the body, while typically rooted in philosopher René Descartes's 17th-century works and called the "Cartesian dualism," has significance for feminist thought because the world of the "mind" has generally been assigned to men (of the dominant class and race) and the world of the "body" has typically been assigned to women (and also to men of lower social status). In this equation, motherwork has been pigeonholed into the realm of the body and talk about mothering focused on what is natural and biological. Thinking, rationality, choosing courses of action that define one's life—these have been seen as the world of men. Feminist writers have worked to shape a more expansive view of women's lives, including mothering, that is characterized by the thinking, rationality, and choosing that have always been inherent to women's experiences. The body/mind dualism infuses another dualism—that between private and public worlds. Historically women have been assigned identity and duties related to the private world of home, and men have been assigned the identity and duties of the public world of work and social congress.

With the separation of men and women into different realms has come the devaluing of the work women do, the purposeful exclusion of women from industry, and an economic dependence that stems from that exclusion. Another problem with this dualism is the isolation that has resulted from women being at home with their children and away from other adult people, conversations, and activities. In the later 1800s, as opportunities for women's education were opening up, beliefs about a gender-based mind/body split were working against those opportunities. Because of women's relegation to the world of the body, a lot of attention was paid to their roles as reproducers, mothers, and domestic caretakers. Little attention, on the other hand, was paid to men as reproducers, fathers, and domestic caretakers; instead they were viewed in terms of their roles as thinkers and competitors in the work world. Some scientists and medical practitioners held that if women pursued intellectual development, their reproductive development would suffer so much that their uteruses would deteriorate.

While we don't see such outlandish arguments operating today, we certainly see residual arguments that women's natural roles as mothers are their primary function and that their energies are properly channeled into the home, even if they also work outside the home or attend school. Though the forms of the arguments are different now, the outcomes are quite similar: Women are still encouraged to focus on domesticity and motherhood at the expense of their intellectual and economic independence. If they are not intellectually independent, women are utterly reliant on the thinking of those who are; they cannot ensure that their best interests are served and, as history has shown, often they aren't. If women are not economically independent, they are utterly reliant on the funding of those who are and, again, they play a

An Evolution of Mother's Day

Mother's Day today is often celebrated as a family's honoring of its mothers. It is a sentimental holiday, not coincidentally marketed to the mass public by the flower, greeting card, and jewelry industries. The profits enjoyed by these industries around Mother's Day depend on the view that the way children and partners can best demonstrate their appreciation to a mother for her self-sacrificing activity all year long is to buy her a simple token of their affection and dote on her for a day. But the origins of Mother's Day were not at all grounded in the sentimental, sometimes hollow emotionalism we and industry assign to it now. In fact, the early concept of Mother's Day in the United States was not even about celebrating and confirming women's roles at home and their contributions to their individual families. It was about celebrating the political power of motherhood and the ways in which mothers organized for the larger society's benefit and for the good of its future generations. It was an effort to push women's influence beyond the realm of home and family and to demonstrate that public and political arenas, and the society at large, were bereft when women's thought and sensibilities were excluded from them.

In the mid-1800s, activist Anna Reeves Jarvis organized Mothers' Work Days in West Virginia, which grew into Mothers' Work Day Clubs. Their purpose was to work in their communities to improve health and sanitary conditions. They assisted mothers stricken with tuberculosis, raised money for medicine, and inspected food and bottled milk. During the Civil War, Jarvis steered the clubs to declare a position of neutrality and to work toward not only caring for soldiers on both sides of the conflict, but

high-stakes gambling game with their best interests and those of their children. The consequent dependence that these two problems instill promotes women's continued lower status in the culture.

Feminist writers have examined the problems of women's isolation in the "private" realm of the home and the resulting limited access to education and earning income in a number of ways. In 1838, Sarah Moore Grimké critiqued the priority placed on young girls' domestic to reconcile communities torn apart by the split between Union and Confederate loyalties. Feminist lecturer, writer, and women's rights activist Julia Ward Howe was similarly disturbed by the ways in which war and violence were tearing nations, families, and individuals apart and was acutely aware of the slaughter, disease, and strife proliferating in the Civil War, as well as the economic devastation that resulted. In response, Howe wrote "Appeal to Womanhood Throughout the World," which came to be known as her "Mother's Day Proclamation." It was a call to mothers everywhere to organize and demand that their nations find nonviolent solutions to national and international problems, that they stop destroying families with war. Soon after, she worked to institute a Mother's Day for Peace, which was celebrated throughout several states until the turn of the century.

The early U.S. Mother's Days were grounded here, in social activism and peace advocacy, and were rooted in the idea of women as social and political activists who benefited society as a whole, rather than as individual contributors to the private lives of single families. When Anna Reeves Jarvis died in 1905, her daughter, also named Anna Jarvis, pledged to establish a nationally recognized Mother's Day. By the time Congress adopted the official holiday in 1914, its meaning had been completely reversed. Seen by politicians, antisuffragists, and merchants as a platform for advancing their own interests, Mother's Day became a consumer-driven and conservative idea that focused exclusively on a privatized view of motherhood that ignored mothers' political contributions and social reform efforts. Today, mother advocacy and feminist groups such as Mothers Acting Up are working to reclaim the political and activist origins of Mother's Day.

training over their studies in her *Letters on the Equality of the Sexes.* And in her 1929 book *A Room of One's Own,* Virginia Woolf discussed the importance of a woman's having her own money, as well as time by herself and not in the service of others, if she is to write and think freely. More recently, Alice Walker's work has called attention to the remarkable and subversive ways that black women have found artistic voice, but she has also pointed to the soul-crushing impact on mothers and their families of having that voice and free thought constricted and impeded by racism.

Some feminists have examined the ways in which women's relegation to the private sphere can turn them into stifled, narrow, frustrated people who are, quite understandably, angry and bitter. In 1792, Mary Wollstonecraft wrote in her *Vindication of the Rights of Woman* that it is important for women "as citizens" to attend to their roles as mothers, but that this duty was *second*. Their first duty, she said, "is to themselves as rational creatures." The exclusion of women from the public, educated, economic sphere rendered them "foolish or vicious." In 1949, French feminist Simone de Beauvoir wrote about the extreme possibility that women, trained to be ill equipped to navigate the public sphere and excluded from all but the mundane world of domesticity, are turned into vapid, irritated people who might be just the kind of people who should *not* be in charge of children. Women might well try to compensate for their frustrations, de Beauvoir argued, by seeking power in the mother-child relationship that is inconceivable elsewhere. It is truly free women, de Beauvoir and many other feminists have reasoned, who can best mother children to live full and liberated lives. In the 1960s, feminist writer and activist Betty Friedan would popularize some of these ideas in her book *The Feminine Mystique*, making them a core element of the women's liberation movement of the 1960s and 1970s.

Working-class women and women of color have argued that the isolation that is characteristic of middle-class white women's lives has not historically been as prevalent for others. Immigrant women of the late 19th century tended to live in tenement housing, comprising two rooms and a kitchen. In these dwellings—a sharp contrast to the former Russian and Irish countrysides they came from—roughly five thousand people lived in a space about the size of a city block, as journalist Gail Collins notes in her book *America's Women*. The problem for these women was not isolation but overcrowding and its resulting disease, as well as the limited opportunity born out of extreme poverty and ethnic segregation.

Black feminist writer Patricia Hill Collins has explained that for black women the boundaries separating families in the private sphere are more fluid. In her book *Black Feminist Thought,* she pointed out that black women have typically relied on woman-centered networks in their domestic and childcare efforts; "bloodmothers" were not expected to be the sole source of sustenance and upbringing for children since mothering has historically been construed in black communities to traverse bloodlines. "Othermothers," represented not only by extended family members but also by community mothering figures, have mediated much of the isolation that is characteristic of white communities. White working-class and poor communities have also relied on this extended network of care, though these communities as a whole may not have afforded the recognition for, and high status to, othermothering that black and other communities of color have.

Women have, of course, always worked outside the home. Working-class and immigrant women and women of color did so long before white middle-class women did, most often as domestic workers and washerwomen for white women—a role that still relegated them to the private world. Discussions about how various kinds of work are divided and how those divisions affect women's lives and result in differences in power and agency have been a continued point of focus for feminist maternal writers. In addition to focusing on issues related to household labor, child rearing, and sharing of childcare in the home and in the community, feminists also have concentrated on issues related to women's paid workforce labor. Specifically, feminists have examined issues such as subsidized childcare as a social issue and not just a women's issue; just compensation for motherwork; equal pay for equal work in the labor force; an equitable split of household labor in dual-career families; and the assumption that children need full-time care from their mothers exclusively. All of these issues have their roots in dualistic divisions between work and home, mind and body, public and private, and "men's work" and "women's work."

While the body/mind and the private/public dualisms have captured the attention of much feminist writing, other dualisms have characterized cultural understandings of mothering as well as feminist responses to them. One of the primary splits examined by feminists has been that between the "good" mother and the "bad" mother. Feminists have looked at how cultural beliefs and attitudes, and more important, economic and political goals, have shaped dominant ideology about good mothering. And they have looked at how that ideology shapes women's own identities as mothers, how women adopt, adapt, or resist its prescriptions. Psychologist and researcher Shari Thurer writes in her book *The Myths of Motherhood* that expectations for mothers have changed drastically through time. For instance, mothers in ancient Egypt and Greece and in Europe during the Middle Ages were supported in a relationship with their children that looks, by comparison to today's, rather disinterested. Many mothers at that time relinquished care of their babies to other women who served as wet nurses. When their children were around, most mothers spent very little time interacting directly with them because the women were often occupied with tasks such as weaving cloth, growing and preparing food, caring for the children of higher-status women, or working as servants. The idea that individual mothers are responsible for the focused upbringing of their individual children is a relatively new phenomenon. In fact, the very *idea* of a "good mother" never even surfaced until the Reformation. This historical variability in what's considered good mothering leads us to question the assumptions that prop up our current thinking about what makes a "good" or "bad" mother.

Contesting Essentialism

Our ideas about women and mothering emerge in part from beliefs about what is at the core, or essence, of motherhood, or in the power of "nature" to determine the shape of motherhood. Beliefs about what is natural for mothers are grounded in a set of assumptions about what is natural for men (so we can assign the opposite to women), what the natural needs of children are, and interestingly, what we believe to be natural in the larger animal kingdom. Just as our notions of what makes a "good" mother have shifted through time, our cultural assumptions about what is "natural" have always been in flux, changing through time according to cultural expectations for families, women, and men. They have also changed according to what is needed to feed the current economic and political system—capitalism in the United States, for example, or feudalism in Europe during the Middle Ages.

A brief look at changing ideas about mothering and childcare will help illustrate how our assumptions are variable and contingent. In the Victorian-era United States, mothers, particularly white, middle-class mothers, were understood to have tender, maternal feelings for their children as part of their female natures. They were self-sacrificing "angels of the house" who were ever-focused on the best interests of others. By the 1940s, mothers' motivations came under suspicion and they were assumed to have a dark underside as part of their natures, which risked the long-term psychological health of children. Throughout much of U.S. history, widely held beliefs indicated that children's natures suited them for care that was divided among family and community members; as long as someone nearby was watching over them, they were fine. But in the early part of the 20th century, things shifted and children were assumed to need primarily their mothers (at least in the middle class). In the 1970s, research showed that children were well suited for care by others as mothers worked, and now many people hold that children are suited well enough for care by others but that mothers need to make up for it later with lavish amounts of time and energy after work and on the weekends.

Yet despite the fact that understandings about women's and men's natures have changed through time and are therefore not fixed, some women's rights activists and feminists have based their arguments in essentialism—in their belief in natural differences between women and men. For example, early women's rights activists argued that because mothering is a natural part of women's lives, provisions ought be made that allow women to pursue their natural mothering function most effectively. Women in the early temperance movement, such as Frances Willard, argued that alcohol should be outlawed because, among other reasons, men's consumption of it threatened family stability. They fought against men's unquestioned privilege of spending all their own and their wives' salaries on liquor, leaving families destitute. Willard and others argued that the "mother heart" was naturally centered on the decent and proper conduct of their families, and they emphasized what they believed was women's divinely ordained role as moral guardians of the family. These activists held that since women are inherently better suited to direct the interests and activities of the family, their arguments should hold sway in politics and the public arena.

More recently, the 1970s saw the development of "cultural feminism," which asserted that men and women are essentially different. Activist Patricia Robinson, an early advocate of cultural feminism, focused her work on an essentialized, spiritual earth mother. Robinson's ideas emerged from black feminism and exalted the black maternal body as a historical source of power. Cultural feminist perspectives, which still operate today, hold that differences between men and women are rooted more deeply in culture than in biology but that women and men are still, at their "essence," different. They suggest, for example, that women are in fact more cooperative and nurturing than men, that a world run by women would be more peaceful, environment friendly, and focused on group cohesion rather than individualism. But essentializing notions such as these suggest that all women are different from all men, and in the same way.

In general, feminism of the 20th and 21st centuries has been skeptical of the assumption that men and women are different in some fundamental way because this idea has been used throughout the centuries to restrict and oppress women. Feminists have argued that the idea that there is a universal core to womanhood—or to motherhood—is problematic because it ignores the very real ways that culture and experience shape women's identities and knowledge. Maternal feminist writers have worked to point out that perceptions have varied about which elements of mothering are grounded in nature and which are learned or shaped through human interaction. Much has been made, for example, of the idea of "maternal instinct," the idea that mothers "just know" what is right for children, that they intuit their needs without even trying and know instinctively how to meet them. Yet studies of postpartum depression indicate that many women interact with their infants without the slightest sense of connection to them. Many women have reported postpartum that they kept expecting some warm, maternal feelings toward their infants to naturally kick in, and when they didn't, these mothers became convinced that they were loathsome, deficient, or unfit mothers. In addition, countless narratives about mothering through the ages have shown that mothers *struggle* to know what is best for their children and often make mistakes (even serious ones), confer with other mothers as they try to figure out how to parent, and learn as they go from their own and other women's parenting experiences and "mistakes." Clearly the assumption that all mothers share a maternal instinct that guides them through the complexities of mothering is flawed.

Still, many of us know women who *do* seem able to predict their children's needs, who do seem to come across as if they "just know" what works best for their children and how best to appeal to them. Sara Ruddick helped to make some feminist sense of this in her landmark essay-turned-book *Maternal Thinking*, in which she countered the idea of maternal instinct. She proposed that mothering practice is a kind of "discipline," a set of skills and ways of thinking that are meticulously *crafted* in interaction with children. So while many women do often have an acute understanding of children and how to care for them, Ruddick argues that this understanding should not be blithely attributed to some sort of biological force grounded in nature, but rather it should be attributed to the very complicated and skilled intellectual and physical labor that characterizes the day-to-day practices of mothering. Understanding women's mothering knowledge to be grounded in *maternal thinking* rather than maternal instinct positions us to consider the concentrated effort that women put into mothering, rather than to assume that it comes to them as quickly and effortlessly as, say, an instinctive "fight or flight" response to danger. The concept of maternal thinking also suggests that "motherly" behavior and knowledge of children's best interests are not merely grounded

Animal Nature and Human Possibility

The animal kingdom is often pointed to as proof that current family and social relationships are "natural" and therefore not subject to change. But the conclusions we draw about human behavior based on other animal behavior depend on which animals and which behaviors we focus on. If we look at primates such as rhesus monkeys or baboons, for example, we might conclude that aggression and competition determine survival and that females choose male mates based on their place in a competitive social hierarchy and do not expect them to perform attentive care toward offspring. And indeed, such primates have been at the center of human and animal comparisons. But a look at different animals would reveal other behaviors. If we were to observe primates such as bonobo chimps, we would likely conclude that cooperation offers a greater likelihood of survival than competition does, and that females choose mates based on high cooperation and low aggression levels and do expect males to take part in caring for offspring.

We could also conclude from observations of bonobos that the communal care of offspring (mothers giving and receiving regular childcare assistance to and from other community members) is much more grounded in nature than individual parents caring for their individual offspring is. We could conclude that the idea of a self-sufficient nuclear family that

in biology. Rather than emerging naturally and exclusively between mothers and their biological children, such behavior and knowledge emerge from purposeful thought and the engaged practice of caring for children. Therefore, adoptive moms, stepmoms, community moms, and other caretakers, as well as biological dads, adoptive dads, stepdads, and others, acquire maternal thinking. Mothering is not, then, the exclusive domain of biological mothers; it is a product of one's disciplined, focused, and persistent *effort*.

Current feminist theory tends to focus largely on the ways that motherhood and experiences of mothering are constructed through social practices. That is, rather than assume that mothering experiences are grounded in biology or nature and are the same for all women, focuses only on its own members is a uniquely human construction (and even then only among some of those humans). If we were to then focus our lens on other animals and draw conclusions about humans from them, we might conclude from penguins, for example, that adult males' tight integration into infant care is natural. We might conclude from dolphins that raising offspring in same-sex groups is natural.

But these are not the animals we usually use as examples when considering human nature, *even though they could be*. Instead, the dominant images from scientific explanations that become part of our own everyday understandings focus a lens sharply on animals that support a very specific social structure—one in which males are dominant and aggressive leaders and females are nurturing followers who are responsible for offspring.

The fact that our assumptions and expectations are culturally variable and contingent on how we direct our observations of other people and other species is not to suggest that they operate with little weight. Indeed, in a given time and place, we treat our assumptions as incontrovertible truths, allowing them to profoundly direct our beliefs and our actions. But if we were to use animal observations as a way of explaining human *possibility*, rather than using them to try and pinpoint human *nature*, we would probably be less committed to the "truth" of observations and more committed to exploring a much greater breadth and variety of human relationships, behaviors, and choices.

feminism typically holds that they are largely shaped by social expectations and norms, dominant assumptions about what makes "good" or "bad" mothers, women's roles and opportunities in their cultures and subcultures, and government (and other institutional) support of different families. Much of the theorizing about motherhood has recognized that, while there may be dimensions of the mother-child relationship that women experience as natural or innate, women have not experienced these dimensions the same way across cultures, through history, and across different family forms. Mothers' diversity of experience indicates that, to a great degree, examinations of motherhood as socially constructed may tell us more about the lives of mothers and children than would considerations of motherhood as natural or innate.

Exploring Intersections of Difference

White middle-class values and practices dictate dominant cultural thinking about how mothers should care for their children. This is evidenced, for instance, through contradictory public dialogue and policy about children's needs. Such dialogue and policy are grounded in conflicting assumptions that, on one hand, young children "need" their mothers out of the workforce and in the home with them, and on the other hand, poor children do not need their mothers at home with them. Poor mothers are coerced to "get to work" by government-assistance policies that require women receiving aid to seek and accept employment—no matter its compensation or work conditions—thus prohibiting them from being at home for their children. So in the issue of ascertaining "children's needs," the question emerges: *Which* children are we referring to? The answer to this question suggests that beliefs about how mothers can best meet children's needs are grounded not in some pure need that all children have, but instead in some desire to regulate different women's lives in different ways so that they serve particular social and political ends.

Because dominant ideas about mothers and children are derived from white, middle-class perspectives and assumptions, it is particularly important in the study and critique of motherhood that feminists widen the lens through which we view mothers' experiences. Although women of a variety of cultures, ethnicities, and classes have participated in feminist movements, they have not received the concentrated focus of research and historical or critical examination that white women have. Further, the women representing nondominant cultures, ethnicities, and classes have faced limited access to and acceptance in academic publication outlets. As a consequence, much of what has been written and published about feminism and motherhood has failed to adequately examine the multiplicity of women's experiences and points of view.

The late 20th and early 21st centuries have seen a proliferation of writing about motherhood, with much more attention to culture and class differences between women than previously. Feminists have concentrated on how views of motherwork are grounded in race and gender biases and on the specific concerns for single mothers. Feminist analyses of differences among mothers still need continued strengthening, and the centering of white middle-class life warrants reconfiguring. But the work of several feminist, womanist, and other writers has begun to "shift the center" of our analysis, to use Patricia Hill Collins's words, and focus on mothers of color as well as lesbian, working-class, and poor mothers.

Catalyzed in part by 1970s writings such as Ti-Grace Atkinson's *Amazon Odyssey,* Jill Johnston's *Lesbian Nation,* and the Combahee River Collective's "A Black Feminist Statement," as well as the 1980s anthology *This Bridge Called My Back: Writings by Radical Women of Color* compiled by Cherríe Moraga and Gloria Anzaldúa, feminist writing has seen an expansion of its limited vision. Alice Walker's 1974 book, *In Search of Our Mothers' Gardens,* is an example of one of the early works that extended discussions about categories of difference to mothering. In it she examines the creative spirit of black women and how, despite racism and oppression, the appreciation for love and beauty and strength is a legacy passed from black mothers to their daughters. Walker's positive view of mothering and of female power in the mother-daughter relationship would prove to be a powerful influence on the feminist writing that would follow in the next decades. Audre Lorde's essay "Man Child: A Black Lesbian Feminist's Response" in her book *Sister Outsider* in 1984 is another example of this early extended discussion. Sandra Pollack and Jeanne Vaughan's 1987 anthology *Politics of the Heart: A Lesbian Parenting Anthology* is a third. These last two works are notable for their effort to move lesbian feminism toward an acceptance of mothering as a viable choice, beyond the outspoken but minority 1960s view of mothering as a sellout to the dominant ideology of the nuclear family and the heterosexual system.

Since the beginning of the 1990s, feminism has paid even greater attention to diversity among women and of family forms. This focus has coincided with a broader pattern in feminism in the later second wave and the overlapping early third wave, as well as in womanist writing and activism, of examining race, class, sexuality, and other aspects of identity, of turning a lens to women's lives globally, and of developing a more inclusive political agenda. In these writings, we see discussions of "intersecting" identities and oppressions. Taking a perspective of intersectionality means understanding that people live multiple identities, that these identities intersect in different ways for different people, and that categories of experience and social status cannot be understood separately from each other because they have a combined effect. People do not face identical obstacles simply because they share a single social status. The paradigm of intersectionality is a response to the framework that views oppression in terms of a hierarchy, which suggests that one form of oppression, such as gender, is more insidious or more fundamental than others.

Intersectionality, now a prominent view in feminist thinking, suggests that my own "social location" or position in society as a woman cannot be accurately understood unless you also consider my location as a member of the educated middle class, and as a white person, as well as my location as a heterosexual and as someone who is middle-aged and able-bodied. I inhabit a very different social location from that which, say, poet Audre Lorde did. Lorde and I were/are both educated women and mothers, but her being lesbian and black situated her very differently from how my being heterosexual and white situates me. She also was less able-bodied than I am, given her severe problems with vision. She experienced life as a renowned and award-winning poet and I have enjoyed no such acclaim, but she also endured sharp criticism as a poet who was black and lesbian and who boldly critiqued both patriarchy and white feminism. Her work, especially as it emerged from her various social locations, was seen as much more of a threat to the dominant ideology than my work on motherhood and feminism, written by someone who is "straight" and white. So to look at Audre Lorde and Amber Kinser monolithically as "women" or "mothers" is to fail to see most of what we each are. To see us even as "educated women" does the same. One would need to note how we are differently situated through race and sexuality and ability and so on to get a clearer sense of who we are and what we face.

This sort of analysis of women's different social locations can be

AN OVERVIEW OF FEMINIST WRITING ON MOTHERHOOD 25

extended to understand how social, economic, and political issues affect different women in very different ways. For instance, feminists have argued, especially since the late 1960s, that a primary culprit in mothers' disempowerment is the unequal distribution of household labor. They contend that women are unfairly burdened because they continue to do 70 percent to 90 percent of the home care, despite changing attitudes about gender roles, and despite the fact that in a majority of two-parent families, both parents work outside the home. But this focus on division of household labor as a major problem for women doesn't make sense for many mothers. Single mothers, for instance, have indicated that their primary problems relate more to poverty and to issues of restricted time. For lesbian mothers, protecting their families from homophobia and working against assumptions of them as unacceptable mothers often are more primary concerns. The 2008 Arkansas Adoption Act, for example, presumes that same-sex couples, who are denied the right to marriage in most states in the United States, are unfit adoptive or foster parents. Facing realities such as this law makes the division of household labor a much less significant issue for queer mothers, for whom gender intersects with sexual identity to create very different experiences of maternal power. If feminism is to work on behalf of all women, it must incorporate an awareness of how race, ethnicity, sexuality, ability, age, and other factors combine to create a unique lived experience for each woman.

Questioning Representations of Mothering

Ideas about mothering are always in flux. At this very moment our ideas are in the process of change. In thirty or forty or fifty years very different models for mothering will likely exist from the ones that surround us right now. In the book *The Way We Never Were* historian Stephanie Coontz discusses the tremendous hold that 1950s-era images of the American family have on our imagination: a financially secure, nuclear, heterosexual, single-breadwinner family, with a mother who was fulfilled exclusively and completely in her domestic role and a father who had a tender disinterest in the workings of the home and only an occasional involvement with the children that was marked by either discipline or play. This image of the "traditional" family has never represented a majority of families; it represented only a certain population, and only for a very restricted period that is now long past. *It was never, in fact, traditional.* Nevertheless, the public imagination for family life is, by many, held captive and captivated by the idea of a "traditional" family that fits this deviant fifties image. At the heart of the good mother/bad mother dualism is a denigration of all that doesn't fit the narrow parameters defined by dominant ideology. So single mothers, lesbian mothers, poor mothers, disabled mothers, young mothers, old mothers, noncustodial mothers, adoptive mothers, divorced mothers, mothers of interracial children or in interracial relationships, and mothers employed full time all struggle against a host of values and expectations that were conceived and continue to be perpetuated without regard for their families. This list represents a formidable number of families; against this list, the "traditional" nuclear family is a minority.

As you read this book, keep in mind feminism's recognition that societal beliefs and attitudes are never set in stone and that women have played and continue to play a critical role in shaping those beliefs and attitudes. The ways we think about motherhood, how different women experience it in different ways, and how it can be made more empowering continue to benefit from feminism's willingness to confront ideas, even when it makes people uncomfortable. You, too, have a part to play in shaping them as you confront ideas in your own way. As you think about what you are reading here and about what your peers, friends, family, and the media are saying about women and mothers, consider some of the following questions: Whose experience of mothering is being talked about? Whose interests does this idea about mothering serve? What assumptions are behind this particular idea about women? How might different assumptions about women or men, or about work, create a different view of family life? How might race, class, or sexuality play into what "gets to count" in the story being told here? Who is being left out of this picture? And finally, how can we make positive changes that will improve the lives of all mothers?

CHAPTER 2

FROM THE MOTHER HEART TO THE MOTHER'S VOTE

THE VICTORIAN ERA, THE INDUSTRIAL REVOLUTION, the Woman's Era, the Progressive Era—all of these "moments" in time combined to make the 19th and early 20th centuries an age of epic change in U.S. history. And each of these periods individually made their indelible marks on families and on motherhood. An examination of these historical eras highlights how the role of the family, the shape of motherhood, and the way that race and class in particular play into them are in large part a function of economics and social power. Family, mothering, and women's experiences of them are intricately interwoven with systems of economic privilege and the systems of economic marginalization that inevitably flow from them. Looking at mothering from a feminist perspective requires persistent considerations of how social stratification influences family life, opportunity, and resources.

A look at what "feminists" were saying and writing about "motherhood" during the 19th century will yield little to examine, especially considering the breadth of the time frame of one hundred years. This is in part because comparatively few women identified with a "feminist" label in these early years. In fact, largely white, middle- and upper-class women (and not a majority of them either) used this label to identify their concerns with gender equity, which rarely took into account issues of class or race. Yet these women were often the ones who attained public visibility and support for the publication of their ideas. It is important then to use a wide-angled lens to view families in this period, looking broadly at women's power and oppression. Otherwise, we end up emphasizing those at upper levels of the social hierarchy and ignoring most everyone else, thereby making little progress toward the feminist goal of achieving equity among all peoples.

Essentialism and the Public/Private Dualism in the Industrial Revolution

Although the Industrial Revolution began in the late 1700s, it became a firmly entrenched force in economic and family life by the 1830s. It marked a momentous shift in the United States from an agrarian and domestic economy to an industry-based one. Before and in the early years of the 1800s, many families' means of making a living were directly tied to home activities, such as farming and in-home production, through which family groups worked together to create food, clothing, and other wares. To get by, families would use these goods themselves or exchange them for items produced by other family groups. In the process, the whole of the family group would raise children—who also were active contributors to the family economy. Women and men often were in charge of different tasks, but the worlds of work and home were interwoven. With the advent of the Industrial Revolution, families were able to buy products that they had previously made or grown themselves, but this necessitated a flow of cash that would enable such purchases. Families in the United States became consuming units instead of producing units, and for many of them that meant going to work in the industries. This shift posed a dilemma for the care of their children, who now would no longer be surrounded by adults and busied in the work of family economics. Mothers and married women, especially of the middle class, came to be seen more exclusively in terms of their domestic and maternal functions and were assigned the "private" realm of home, as men were assigned the "public" realm of work outside it.

With this shift in family life and industry emerged the belief that women should be solely in charge of the home and the children. Since then, mothering and domesticity have been intimately tied. This gender-based split between public and private realms is referred to as the "separate spheres" ideology. Of course, the two spheres were not actually separate, since what happened in the public realm, such as the earning of income and the making of policy, profoundly affected what happened in the private realm. Also, the divide that did exist between public and private realms mostly applied to wealthy or middle-class white families; poor and working-class families and immigrant and Native families rarely lived as if the two spheres were separate.

Women's changing responsibility for the home was, in the 19th century, compounded by changing expectations for parenting children. Childhood, especially white, middle-class childhood, came to be seen as a unique period in the life cycle that required a special kind of nurturing and guidance. In the 17th and 18th centuries, views of childhood had generally been based on Calvinist beliefs that children were born sinful and in need of correction. Parents had been advised to raise their children together, often led by the father, in ways that shut down their inherent corruption. But these views of children as naturally evil—views that Native communities, for example, did not share—gave way in the 19th century to the idea of "tabula rasa," or children as a "blank slate," waiting to be molded. These innocents looked to adults, especially mothers, to model for them strong moral grounding and to provide experiences that would help them shape their characters. How children turned out would no longer be blamed on inherent and sinful corruption. The building of a child's—and future citizen's—moral character, industriousness, and self-discipline was now the sole responsibility (and blame) of the mother. A mother was expected to pour all her energy into molding children and creating a home that was the moral center of the family and the community.

This was a time that exalted motherhood, especially among middle-class and wealthy whites, often employing a kind of dripping sentimentality to discussions of women's roles and "home sweet home." Such exaltation emerged partly to counter the aggressive and competitive world brought about by industrialization: The mother's devotion and care would not only direct childhood, but it would also prepare children to honorably navigate the world of commerce without adopting its unscrupulous worldview. This arrangement, of course,

Activists Challenge Idea of Separate Spheres

Newspapers responded to the first women's rights convention in 1848 at Seneca Falls, New York, with a fervor. Headlines such as "Insurrection Among Women" and "Women Out of Their Latitude" reveal the flavor of their responses. Conference attendees were called "Amazons" who "demoralize and degrade from their high sphere and noble destiny" through claims for suffrage that were "defective." In this excerpt, featured in the *National Reformer* in Rochester, New York, convention leader and primary philosopher of the "first wave" feminist movement Elizabeth Cady Stanton responded to the news hype. In particular, she critiqued the popular conception of women's sphere in the "private" realm and men's in the "public." Stanton makes the bold declaration here that women will decide for themselves which sphere is appropriate for different times in their lives.

There is no such thing as a sphere for a sex. Every man has a different sphere, and one in which he may shine, and it is the same with every woman; and the same woman may have a different sphere at different times. The distinguished Angelina Grimké was acknowledged by all the anti-slavery host to be in her sphere, when, years ago, she went

allowed the problems of industrialization to continue unchecked, since mothers would presumably neutralize them. Working-class and poor mothers and mothers of color, whose family members were relegated to the least desirable and most exploitive of occupations, if they were fortunate enough to find work at all, were expected by dominant culture to meet the impossible task of offsetting the worst excesses of industry and, as if that weren't enough, to provide moral uplift in the process. Because such a task was insurmountable, they were often labeled "bad mothers." Here lay the seeds of a dualism of the exalted "good" mother and the scorned "bad" mother that would take increasingly agitating forms in the 20th and 21st centuries. The 19th-century exaltation of *through the length and breadth of New England, telling the people of her personal experience of the horrors and abominations of the slave system, and by her eloquence and power as a public speaker, producing an effect unsurpassed by any of the highly gifted men of her day. Who dares to say that in thus using her splendid talents in speaking for the dumb, pleading the cause of the poor friendless slave, that she was out of her sphere? Angelina Grimké is now a wife and the mother of several children. We hear of her no more in public. Her sphere and her duties have changed. She deems it her first and her most sacred duty to devote all her time and talents to her household and to the education of her children. We do not say that she is not now in her sphere. The highly gifted Quakeress, Lucretia Mott, married early in life, and brought up a large family of children. All who have seen her at home agree that she was a pattern as a wife, mother, and housekeeper. No one ever fulfilled all the duties of that sphere more perfectly than did she. Her children are now settled in their own homes. Her husband and herself, having a comfortable fortune, pass much of their time in going about and doing good. Lucretia Mott has now no domestic cares. She has a talent for public speaking; her mind is of a high order; her moral perceptions remarkably clear; her religious fervor deep and intense; and who shall tell us that this divinely inspired woman is out of her sphere in her public endeavors to rouse this wicked nation to a sense of its awful guilt, to its great sins of war, slavery, injustice to woman and the laboring poor.*

motherhood also emerged in response to the fact that the home was no longer a locus of manufacture and subsistence activity, so aggrandizing and complicating motherhood helped make sense of many women's reduced productivity at home. It also served the purpose, as historian Paula Giddings points out in *When and Where I Enter: The Impact of Black Women on Race and Sex in America,* of helping men to restrict women's activity since the men were no longer always present at home and to ensure women's submission and loyalty since the women were no longer equal contributors to the family economy.

Outside of the industrialized centers, plantation economies shaped the family lives of slave owners as well as those of enslaved people. In

JUST LIKE JOAN OF ARC
The Anti-Suffragist Has a "Vision" of Her Duty

This 1915 cartoon depicts the anti-suffragist as a woman who adheres to the prevalent belief from the previous century that women should avoid the corrupting influence of the male world of politics.

the North and the South, an abundance of currency freed upper-class women and men from the drudgery of the tasks of everyday living, but it then created expectations that someone else would be employed to do such tasks for them. Populations increased in the United States much faster than industry jobs did, and since white men were chosen first for better-paying jobs, those who were left to do the menial tasks of the rich were the poor and ethnically marginalized. Multiple industries created products and services that were marketed to middle-class consumers but that also shaped a new standard of living against which most people were judged.

In a similar way, the standards and views directing women's and men's roles at work and at home were grounded in white, middle-class values, but they quite frequently were used to determine the competence and desirability of other mothers. White culture doubted, at best, the very humanity of some mothers, including enslaved women, free black women, and Native women, who all lived with the stigma of being considered less than full persons. So even though widespread assumptions about the sanctity of childhood and the home, and feminine dependence and submissiveness, required that mothers remain out of the workforce and devote themselves wholly to home and hearth, such assumptions did not apply to nonwhite families and homes in the same way. The ability of other mothers to create a sanctuary for their families was of no apparent concern to the middle or upper classes, or to the industries that favored white workers at their middle and upper levels. Similarly, the ability of poor immigrant women to focus exclusively on creating a pristine home and raising "pure" children untainted by the harsh outside world was rendered impossible by class restrictions. While many immigrant families supported the idea that once women married they should leave the public world of work and attend to home and children, many immigrant women nevertheless continued to find ways to earn income by working at home, sewing garments for pay by the piece or taking boarders into their already crowded homes. Others worked in the factories—the darkest recesses of industrial society. All of these women were able to devote little time to their children. And still, the middle-class ideology of womanhood—variously called the cult of domesticity, the cult of true womanhood, and the cult of pure motherhood—created the standards against which all women were judged by white culture, and sometimes by themselves. Typically, women of color and poor white women were found wanting, even though it was largely their labors, in domestic service, for example, that freed wealthy and middle-class women to meet those standards. It was upon the backs of these women, and men, that the cult of domesticity stood.

In many Native cultures women experienced no "split" between work and home, since these spheres were one and the same. Native American scholar and advocate Barbara Alice Mann explains in her book *Iroquoian Women* that for the Iroquois, women were considered the *core* of public involvements. Mothers were not solely responsible for their children; children were of the community and child rearing was shared among community members. Family activity and subsistence activity were enjoined, and rather than be exalted for being mothers of their children or makers of their homes, Iroquois females were valued for being women in their own right. Because they were esteemed as women, they were central to the governing, familial, spiritual, and economic activities of the group. Little is said in early feminist writings from Native women's perspectives, partly because Native women did not record their lives in the printed forms that white women used, but largely because they did not need a way to gain power, status, and value in their culture.

Little also was said in early feminist writings from the perspective of African American women. This too was due partly to black women's restricted use of or access to the printed word, but also largely to the ways that gender relations in black families did not facilitate similar kinds of inequities between women and men as they emerged from slavery. Some writers have argued that slave women and men showed little gender distinction in family life because they were oppressed in similar ways. In contrast, black feminist researcher Bonnie Thornton Dill argued in her article "Our Mothers' Grief" that there was in fact a gendered division of family labor. Enslaved women were the first to experience the "double day"—similar to what feminists refer to today as the "second shift"—a shift of household and child rearing labor that began only after a full day of slave labor. Dill explained, however, that this gender distinction, while problematic, was different from what white couples experienced because it was not wrapped up in the male partner's higher status and subjugation of the female partner. Dill also has shown that when black slave families moved to sharecropping after slavery, they experienced a complementarity of tasks in their labor, much as white families did in preindustrial society. Though black couples did not experience the same economic independence as preindustrial white couples did, gendered labor roles were similarly equitable.

Women's rights activists, many of whom were white feminists, responded to the ways that women experienced family life and motherhood. But given the extent to which motherhood was glorified and sentimentalized in this period, they understandably did not write and speak out against motherhood itself. They did not question whether motherhood was a necessary part of a woman's life or critique the burdens of child rearing or advocate for workplace equality. Instead, they used motherhood as the platform for a host of other arguments. In the main, these arguments were twofold. First, they held that women's natural suitability for maternal care and the moral uplift of their families and communities made them naturally suited for much broader public activity. For example, in her popular 1852 novel *Uncle Tom's Cabin,* Harriet Beecher Stowe grounded appeals to her readers in what came to be a frequently used "mother heart" argument to advocate for antislavery sentiment and activism. Stowe portrayed the white mother in her novel as naturally able to relate, through their common maternal experience, to the plight of the black slave mother in search of her son who had been sold away from her. Indeed, the common belief among white women in their natural maternal capacity to exert their moral influence and to advocate for those less able to advocate for themselves was used and maneuvered to the advantage of the abolitionist movement. Because motherhood defined women, according to the dominant beliefs of the time, woman activists used it to pursue myriad other activities and platforms, including the suffrage, temperance, women's club, and settlement house movements.

Second, women's rights activists held that increased rights as citizens would help women to be better mothers. They argued for guardianship of their children even after divorce on the grounds that they could better mother them, and they argued that they should have property rights on the grounds that they could then offer safer haven to their children. Even Mary Wollstonecraft's landmark 1792 work *A Vindication of the*

Rights of Woman, which is often noted as the European precursor to the American women's rights movement, argued for women's right to education beyond domestic training in large part because it would make them better mothers: "To be a good mother—a woman must have sense, and that independence of mind which few women possess who are taught to depend entirely on their husbands. . . . Unless the understanding of woman be enlarged, and her character rendered more firm, by being allowed to govern her own conduct, she will never have sufficient sense to command or temper to manage her children more properly." Other activists promoted education as a way to enhance the execution of a woman's maternally grounded role in the community as nurturer and moral compass. That this argument was widely used should not be read to mean that it was widely accepted. In fact, many women and men were opposed outright to women venturing beyond the confines of the home, lest they be corrupted by the ruthless world outside and not only potentially bring that callous mind-set back to the home, hearth, and community, but also fail in their responsibility to purge it from men's lives.

Other opponents of women's education used different arguments against it. In 1874, Dr. Edward H. Clarke's influential book *Sex in Education* made a case against women's education on the grounds that it caused deterioration of the uterus. Indicating that women's and men's bodies operated on limited resources, Clarke argued that a body could foster growth in only one area—either brains or reproductive organs, but not both. For men, that meant hoarding their reproductive energy for the sake of developing the mind and the healthy drive toward competition so necessary in industry; for women, that meant shunning anything intellectual in order to preserve reproductive function. Armed with Clarke's apparent medical backing, doctors of the time stridently campaigned against women's education. But feminists such as Mary Wollstonecraft, Emma Goldman, and others fought back.

The Education Debates

In *Sex in Education*, Dr. Edward H. Clarke claimed that the female body is appropriately but singularly directed toward reproductive function, and that it must not be distracted from that or depleted by rigorous educational demands. Girls should be allowed to learn at home, or in specialized educational environments that allow for learning in short spurts and long rest periods that correspond with the menstrual cycle. Such a schedule would allow the female body to recover between periods of study, thus "obeying" the "periodicity" of their physiological "organization." Colleges in the United States, then, which offered no such flexibility in their regimens, were attended at the great expense of the mental health and reproductive capacity of America's future wives and mothers. In short, formal education would "arrest the development of the reproductive apparatus," resulting in a wide array of potential problems: "The educational methods of our schools and colleges of girls are, to a large extent, the cause of 'the thousand ills' that beset American women. . . . It has been reserved for our age and country, by its methods of female education, to demonstrate that it is possible in some cases to divest a woman of her chief feminine functions; in others, to produce grave and even fatal disease of the brain and nervous system; in others to engender torturing derangements and imperfections of the reproductive apparatus that imbitter a lifetime." Clarke offered little support for these claims, other than a few case studies from his own practice.

Feminists and women's rights activists argued back. Julia Ward Howe's answer to Clarke came in the form of the book *Sex and Education: A Reply to Dr. E. H. Clarke's "Sex in Education,"* in which she collected responses from various notable figures and testimony from several women's colleges and coeducational universities (Vassar, Antioch, Oberlin, and Michigan and Lombard Universities) attesting to the fact that female students do *not* show increased signs of ill health and sharply disputing the connection Clarke draws between the rigors of college and reproductive health and function. Following are two excerpts from Howe's collection:

continued

continued from previous page

From author and feminist Elizabeth Stuart Phelps:

> *Thousands of women will not believe what the author of "Sex in Education" tells them, simply because they know better. . . . Women sick because they study? Does it not look a little more as if women were sick because they stopped studying? . . . Let us draw upon our imagination to the extent of inquiring whether the nineteenth-century girl . . . might not be made an invalid . . . by exchanging the wholesome pursuit of sufficient and worthy aims for the unrelieved routine of a dependent domestic life, from which all aim has departed . . . made an invalid by the prejudice that deprives her of the stimulus which every human being needs and finds in the pursuit of some one especial avocation, and confines that avocation for her to a marriage which she may never effect, and which may never help the matter if she does. Made an invalid by the change from doing something to doing nothing. . . . Made an invalid, in short for just the reasons . . . why a man would be made an invalid if subjected to the woman's life when the woman's education is over.*

From writer Maria A. Elmore, who speaks here on behalf of working women, critiquing Clarke's middle-class bias:

> *Does that regimen which men are ever prescribing for women, namely marriage, grant her one week's cessation from labor out of every four? Can a mother, when weary and over-tasked, relinquish the work and care of her family, and engage her thoughts upon nothing save that of her own physical weaknesses, and how to relieve them? No, women may work in the factory, in the store, in the workshop, in the field, in the dining saloon, at the wash-tub, at the ironing-table, at the sewing-machine—do all these things, and many more equally hard, from Monday morning till Saturday night every week in the year; may wear their lives out toiling for their children, and doing the work for their families that their husbands ought to do, and nobody raises the arm of opposition; but just now, because there is a possibility and even probability that in matters of education women will be as honorably treated as men, lo! Dr. Clarke comes forth and tells us it ought not be so, because, forsooth, the periodical tides and reproductive apparatus of her organization will be ignored!*

Change in the Progressive Era
Science, Race, and the Good/Bad Mother

During the period of the late 1800s and early 1900s—often labeled the Progressive Era, and called the "Woman's Era" by black female activists—the focus on mothering as character formation was supplanted by a focus on "scientific mothering." Women were now expected to depend on childhood and parenting "experts" who insisted that mothers needed training and study to mother effectively. As in the 17th century, children were seen again as potentially dangerous. But this time the danger came not from children's inherent sinfulness but from their natural "drives" or impulses that needed to be restrained through rigid scheduling, detached discipline, and strict adherence to expert advice. Mothers were cautioned against the negative outcomes of "smother love"; too much affection and not enough regimen would produce children and future citizens who were dismal failures. And for such failures, once again children and government and the larger society had no one but mothers to blame.

In the Progressive Era, as earlier in the 19th century, motherhood was tightly entwined with domesticity. Housework, cleaning, and child rearing all required regimen, meticulous attention to detail, and a substantial amount of mothers' time and energy.

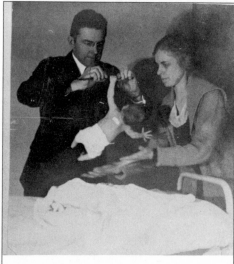

Grasping Reflex. Present from birth to approximately 121 days (limits not yet determined).

I.Johns Hopkins University Archives

In the early 20th century, mothers were expected to rely on the advice of parenting experts, who emphasized discipline, regimen, and restraint. Here, John B. Watson, an early proponent of behavioral psychology, tests the grasp reflex in a baby.

Those mothers who could afford it employed the domestic service of other women—working-class white women and women of color—and thus were "free" to spend more concentrated energy on developing the minds and spirits of their children. On the other hand, poor women were seldom in a position to devote much of their day to children, since they were devoting so much of it already to trying to survive. The kinds of mothering advocated so stridently by the experts was, not surprisingly, antithetical to poor and working-class life. Even among the middle class, the expectation that women always keep abreast of the latest developments in domestic and child rearing science was overwhelming, and it ensured that many women's lives extended no further than their homes. The scientific "proof" that all mothering should take particular and time-consuming forms to be acceptable and improve the stock of the U.S. citizenry resulted in activist and government efforts to intervene in the lives of those who did not or could not meet the systematic standards of the day.

In the Progressive Era, motherhood also began to be framed as a distinctly racial duty. Both black and white women were inculcated into the belief that they were responsible for mothering not just their own children, or their community's children, but their entire race. In 1906, President Theodore Roosevelt, responding to the declining white middle-class birth rate, accused white women of committing the "sin" of "race suicide." They were admonished for being self-serving, for not embracing their national duty to be mothers of the nation. This accusation fit well with the ideas of scientific child rearing—if white women could be convinced that child rearing was so complex an endeavor that it could function as a woman's sole occupation and future, then the country need not worry that she might make decisions about the size of her family based on her desire to pursue some other occupation or avocation. And, more important, Anglo populations could continue to outnumber and remain dominant over populations of color. Black women, on the other hand, were incriminated by dominant culture with claims that they were having more children than their lesser incomes and their presumed limited knowledge about proper (scientific) mothering could handle. Simultaneously, they were charged by their own communities with the responsibility of "racial uplift," of holding the future of the race in their hands.

The increased emphasis on fastidious and painstaking mothering practices, and the relationship between mothering and race obligation in this era, point to a primary operating principle of the time, which informed women's activist efforts as well as political rhetoric and government policy regarding families. Although everyday discourse was still guided by the assumption of public and private spheres as separate, women challenged this assumption by focusing their attention on the public realm and how it ought to be more invested in citizens' private lives. As the 20th century wore on, this principle would eventually supersede women's 19th-century focus on finding ways that their private-life roles, such as taking care of others, ought to extend into the public realm. But in the decades surrounding the turn of the century, women were still working to establish their place in the public realm as mothers.

Blurring Distinctions Between Public and Private

In the late 1800s, the widespread obsessive focus on maternity, coupled with the ways in which women of color saw their oppressions as intruding from outside their families rather than emerging from within them, made it unlikely that women thought about mothering as oppressive. Instead, feminists and women's rights activists argued that limiting women's capacities to the care of children was unwise for the nation. In 1892, Anna Julia Cooper, the self-declared black "voice from the South," in her book by the same name, wrote about women's role in the public, political arena. Echoing sentiments from earlier in the century, Cooper argued that woman's power in that arena emerged from her essential difference from man—her moral grounding—which guided her vision for "the happiness of homes and the righteousness of the country." Similarly, early suffragists argued that women were naturally predisposed to make sound voting decisions because they would make them from their inherently maternal perspective. If women were to be the moral center of the family, they explained, they must be positioned to vote for candidates and policies that were spiritually sound and, to use a more modern phrase, family friendly. In a speech delivered in 1893, white suffragist Carrie Chapman Catt employed the often-used notion of the "mother heart," echoing Harriet Beecher Stowe forty years earlier. Catt claimed that women were asking for no rights that they weren't naturally equipped to execute: "To women have been given in greater perfection the gentler traits of tenderness and mercy, the mother heart, which goes out to the wronged and afflicted everywhere, with the longing to bring them comfort and sympathy and help." Moreover, Catt argued that confining to the home women's natural abilities for understanding the plight and needs of others would rob the citizenry of assets destined to make the nation great. Like Catt, English feminist and writer Julia Wedgwood asserted in 1889 that the "inheritance of maternity in all women" (whether they have children or not) means that woman was the "elder" to man in issues of morality, that she had "a richer material for justice" than he had, and therefore the broader society had need of her naturally imbued qualities in public arenas.

Jane Addams was another feminist who argued against the confinement of female qualities to the home. Perhaps the most famous social worker in U.S. history and the first American woman to win the Nobel Peace Prize, Addams was renowned for establishing Hull-House in Chicago in 1889. Hull-House was the first of what would be many settlement houses in the United States designed to help impoverished immigrants. Specifically, settlement houses served to elevate poor people by providing them with education, recreation, and culture for living a full life; childcare to relieve mothering burdens and allow women to work; and practical vocational training for securing better employment. Addams argued in a 1910 *Ladies' Home Journal* article that marginalized mothers, such as those living in tenement housing, had a justifiable need for access to political power.

> *In a crowded city . . . if the street is not cleaned by the city authorities no amount of private sweeping will keep the tenement free from grime; . . . a tenement-house mother may*

see her children sicken and die of diseases from which she alone is powerless to shield them, although her tenderness and devotion are unbounded. She cannot even secure untainted meat for her household . . . unless the meat has been inspected by city officials. . . . [I]f woman would keep on with her old business of caring for her house and rearing her children she will have to have some conscience in regard to public affairs lying quite outside of her immediate household. . . . [She] must take part in . . . legislation which is alone sufficient to protect the home from the dangers incident to modern life.

Addams also lobbied for legislation that would mandate schooling for children and limit the working hours for women and mothers, and later for women's right to vote. Although Addams's work was well known and highly valued by many, her arguments about restricting women's working hours were resisted by some feminists and other writers. Anthropologist Elsie Clews Parsons, for example, argued that to accede to "protective legislation" (limited working hours is one example), even for mothers, was to acknowledge and perpetuate women's inferior status.

Many activists who were working to cultivate women's political power, particularly as they worked on the campaign for the vote, used images connected with motherhood and domesticity in the messages they spoke and those they distributed such as posters, leaflets, pamphlets, and postcards. These persuasive campaign messages featured the language of "social housekeeping," "cleaning up politics" and taking care of the nation as their larger "home," in addition to more general statements about needing political voice to effectively perform their duty to home and children. For the most part, this approach toward women's political power was adopted by the National American Woman Suffrage Association (NAWSA). Other suffrage leaders who championed the motherhood angle include Anna Howard Shaw, Ida Husted Harper, and Alice Stone Blackwell. These and other NAWSA suffragists used publications such as *The Woman Citizen* and the *Woman's Journal* to advance their platform and get their ideas into

THE DIRTY POOL OF POLITICS

CAN WE CLEAN IT?

GIVE US A CHANCE!

BRIBERY

FOOD ADULTERATION

WHITE SLAVERY

CRAFT

BALLOT

Published by Votes-for-Women Publishing Co., Wilson Bldg., 127 Montgomery St., San Francisco   217

Smithsonian Institution

Like much prosuffrage propaganda, this postcard uses images of women's domestic capabilities to promote their participation in politics.

the hands of the public. Their approach to arguing for the ballot stood in contrast to the more radical suffrage group, the National Women's Party, which focused on women's equal status with men and on the right to individual freedom and power.

In addition to members of the National Women's Party, other women argued outside the framework of woman's nature, though they were far fewer than those who used essentialist arguments. One was Olive Schreiner, a white South African novelist and feminist writer who was especially influential for radical feminists of the time. Her internationally famous novel, *The Story of an African Farm*, not only portrayed a mother as *not* possessing the "mother heart," tenderness, or compassion, but also portrayed father figures as possessing these qualities instead. Her work suggested that motherhood could spell doom for women. Another exception was women's rights activist, critic, and journalist Margaret Fuller, whom Susan B. Anthony, Matilda Joslyn Gage, and Elizabeth Cady Stanton lauded as the person who had a more profound influence on American thought than any woman before her. Fuller's book *Woman in the Nineteenth Century* boldly critiqued gender binaries. She asserted that differences between women and men were culturally produced rather than innate or "natural," which flew in the face of not only the dominant social structure, but also most of the feminist platform. Fuller argued that any division of labor that impedes a woman in developing her full human "soul" by restricting her access to education and occupation beyond the home was detrimental to society as a whole and to women and men individually. A third feminist arguing outside the gender binary framework was Emma Goldman, who resisted mightily any restriction on individual freedom—no matter the platform from which it emerged—and reacted against the "absurd notion" of a "dualism of the sexes," even as she spoke out against what she saw as the narrow scope of feminist emancipation. She refuted arguments that women were inherently maternal or moral, that they were divinely or innately suited to "purify politics," and that an occupation would emancipate them or release them from home drudgery. She also rejected any suggestion that being a lover, or a mother, necessarily made women subordinate. Goldman's ideas have been recognized as visionary and more in synch with those of feminism of the "second wave" than with those of her own time.

Power, Agency, and Community Change

The Progressive Era saw a surge of women's activism more focused and more far-reaching than in any previous period. Activists and policymakers alike were embracing the principle of the time that private lives were of public concern, an idea that was reinforced by the sharpened focus on citizenship and strengthening the nation that accompanied the period surrounding World War I. In addition to those arguing for women's right to vote and for generally extending the role of maternity into the public realm, two primary groups of activists emerged in this era whose work affected mothering and families: the black women's club movement and the white maternalist movement.

Ahead of Her Time

Charlotte Perkins Gilman, a primary feminist voice and prolific author in the late 19th century, wrote pointedly against women's relegation to the home and most critically about the structure of motherhood at the time. In her 1898 book, *Women and Economics*, she critiqued the hypocrisy of referring to women's role as solely or even primarily "maternal," when in fact less of their activity was focused on child rearing than on home care and tending to men. Relatedly, she criticized the double day that many women executed at home and on behalf of the community without due recognition: "We see the human mother worked far harder than a mare, laboring her life long in the service, not of her children only, but of men; husbands, brothers, fathers, whatever male relatives she has; for mother and sister also; for the church a little, if she is allowed; for society, if she is able; for charity and education and reform,—working in many ways that are not the ways of motherhood."

Gilman further critiqued a family and social structure that excluded a (white middle-class) woman from the workforce or loaded her with so much domestic work that she could not take on an additional job, and then denied her independence "on the ground that motherhood prevents her working!" Her aim was to reveal these cultural myths and foster a more honest articulation of all it was that women were doing under the guise of motherhood. If it were true that mothers were too busy with child rearing to pursue other activities—educational or occupational—then, she declared: "We should find a world full of women who never lifted a finger save in the service of their children, and of men who did *all* the work

Black women's clubs largely comprised middle-class black women who took as their mission the "uplift" of the race. Recognizing that middle-class values were those most revered and influential, these women sought to infuse poor and working-class black communities with them, training women on the appropriate exercise of those values. Though club organizers and leaders have been criticized for perpetuating a formerly white worldview and eclipsing African American cultural practices, they also were revered for their commitment to improving besides, and waited on the women whom motherhood prevented from waiting on themselves."

Gilman was one of the few feminists of her time who spoke out against mothers raising children in isolation, claiming that isolating women and giving them no opportunities for development beyond the domestic realm not only debased women but also created crippled mothers in a sense. It posed a danger, she said, not only for children when young, but also for them as future citizens. Gilman's solution, in part, was communal raising of children, including community design in which common kitchens joined separate homes and workers could be employed to do the cooking and meal prep and cleanup. Aleksandra Kollontai, a Russian activist and contemporary of Gilman, agreed that community childcare was necessary for women, especially of the working class. She argued that it would help transform the public and private spheres by enabling them to join the labor movement and work alongside men in it as well as in the workforce.

Even though Gilman sided with some of the prominent views among feminists, she found few supporters among middle-class white women—feminist or not. Because many black, immigrant, and Native women were already engaged in communal rearing of children, Gilman's ideas were likely associated with lower-status families. And given the high esteem in which both mother-only child rearing and methodical domestic work was held, it is not surprising that her ideas were not well received. Swedish feminist Ellen Key, for example, condemned Gilman's ideas, branding her "amaternal" and declaring that it was egregious to suggest anything other than that a woman is most satisfied and most useful, "for her own part most free and for others most fruitful," in the direct activity of caring for children.

the communities, resources, opportunities, and education of black women and their families. Grounded in the belief that, because of black women's central position in their families and communities, to take care of the women is to take care of the race, clubwomen effected monumental change. In fact, to claim home and community as black women's rightful domain was a way to resist dominant white cultural views, which still did not assume, so soon after abolition, the full humanity of black people. To take up the rhetoric of "true womanhood" and naturally maternal qualities was not simply an assimilation into the white world; it functioned as a daring platform for black women, whose right to nurturing, maternal identity and the ability to attend to family and home maintenance had been denied for so long. Adopting Mary Church Terrell's motto "Lifting as We Climb," clubwomen focused on moral and educational reform in their communities. A leader in the black women's club movement, Terrell founded the National Association of Colored Women (NACW) in 1896 with Anna Julia Cooper and Mary Jane Patterson. Clubwomen rarely identified as "feminist." Even so, black historian Deborah Gray White indicates in her recent book *Too Heavy a Load* that the NACW insistence that only black women could save the black race was "unprecedentedly feminist."

Before the end of the century the NACW would boast two hundred clubs, and within the association's first twenty years it would grow to fifteen hundred clubs nationwide. Believing that women's action was core to the future of their race, repressed as it was and hit hard by industrialization, black clubwomen focused on helping communities to be a well-resourced fount of race progress and helping women to assume leadership in that effort. The NACW and its numerous affiliate local clubs comprised multiple service divisions and projects, including domestic science, mothers' meetings, girls' clubs, libraries, rescue work, enrichment classes, temperance efforts, and settlement houses that provided job referrals, childcare, and education. Clubwomen practiced a kind of "social motherhood" that strengthened their communities, even as they helped mothers achieve particular standards of excellence for home and childcare. Embedded in club efforts was an understanding that many black women would have to negotiate home and family maintenance with working outside their homes for a living. Black clubwomen saw "working" mothers as worthy mothers.

While some clubwomen, such as Margaret Murray Washington, saw the home sphere—which for black women already included community—as their sole focus, others, such as Fannie Barrier Williams, saw clubwomen's rightful focus to be broader and to include

Black women's clubs worked to improve their communities through education and outreach to other women. Here, members of the Phyllis Wheatley Club are photographed outside the Michigan Avenue Baptist Church in Buffalo, New York.

involvement in politics, law, and public policy. Williams believed that the black mother's role in particular warranted pointed attention in public policy. But no matter which end of the spectrum black clubwomen represented, they believed that racial uplift was centrally grounded in the home and that race progress was dependent upon black women's initiative in helping black women and families.

A second powerful force in women's activism related to mothering was the activity of white maternalist reformers. These women exerted powerful influence in the development of public policy that spoke to the needs of mothers and children and in the creation of the programs and institutions that would address them. Like black reformers, white maternalists emphasized the importance of motherhood to the larger society. And while they worked to extend women's sphere of influence beyond the domestic, they simultaneously affirmed women's traditional role as mothers. Linking good mothering with the production of good

"In Union There is Strength"

In 1897 Mary Church Terrell, the first president of the National Association of Colored Women, delivered her first address before the organization. In it, she weaved together the ideals of race unity and social motherhood. In this excerpt, she tapped into the idea of women as naturally attentive to the needs of the afflicted, and therefore socially obligated to attend to the afflictions that confronted black people. Terrell centered the hope of the race in the social action of black women.

In Union there is strength is a truism that has been acted upon by Jew and Gentile, by Greek and Barbarian, by all classes and conditions alike from the creation of the universe to the present day. . . . Acting upon this principle of concentration and union have the colored women of the United States banded themselves together to fulfill a mission to which they feel peculiarly adapted and especially called. . . . Believing that it is only through the home that a people can become really good and truly great, the N.A.C.W. shall enter that sacred domain to inculcate right principles of living and correct false views of life. Homes, more homes, purer homes, better homes, is the text upon which our sermons to the masses must be preached. So long as the majority of people call that place home in which the air is foul, the manners bad, and the morals worse, just so long is this so called home a menace to health, a breeder of vice, and the abode of crime. . . . It is, therefore, into the home, sisters of the Association, that we must go, filled with all the zeal and charity which such a mission demands. To the children of the race we owe, as women, a debt which can never be paid, until Herculean efforts are made to rescue them from evil and shame for which they are in no way responsible. Listen to the cry of the children, my sisters. Upon you they depend for the light of knowledge, and the blessing of a good example. As an organization of women, surely nothing can be nearer our hearts than the children, many of whose lives so sad and dark we might brighten and bless. . . .

Through mother meetings which have been in the past year and will be in the future a special feature of the Association, much useful informatics in everything pertaining to the home will be disseminated. Object lessons in the best way to sweep, to dust, to cook and to wash should be given by women who have made a special study of the art and science of housekeep. How to clothe children neatly, how to make, and especially how to mend garments, how to manage their households economically, what food is the most nutritious and best for the money, how to ventilate as thoroughly as possible the dingy stuffy quarters which the majority are forced to inhabit . . . all these are subjects on which the women of the masses need more knowledge. Let us teach mothers of families how to save wisely. Let us have heart to heart talks with our women that we may strike at the root of evil. If the women of the dominant race with all the centuries of education, refinement, and culture in back of them, with all their wealth of opportunity ever present with them, if these women felt a responsibility to call a Mother's Congress that they might be ever enlightened as to the best methods of rearing children and conducting their homes, how much more do the women of our race from whom the shackles of slavery have just fallen need information on the same subjects? Let us have Mother Congresses in every community in which our women can be counseled. . . . Let us not only preach, but practice race unity, race pride, reverence, and respect for those capable of leading and advising us. Let the youth of the race be impressed about the dignity of labor and inspired with a desire to work. Let us do nothing to handicap children in the desperate struggle for existence in which their unfortunate condition in this country forces them to engage. Let us purify the atmosphere of our homes till it become so sweet that those who dwell in them will have a heritage more precious than great, ere to be desired than silver or gold.

citizens and a stronger America, maternalists shaped public policy in ways that reverberate today. Such policy was predicated on a notion of "universal" motherhood, which assumed that white, middle-class perspectives and practices were applicable to all families and in the best interests of all children. This narrowly defined vision of good American motherhood, advocated by policy activists such as Florence Kelley, Julia Lathrop, S. Josephine Baker, and Grace Abbott, was rooted in the perceived truths emerging at that time from the fields of psychology, medicine, and social work.

Maternalists were central to the creation in the early 1900s of a welfare state, a set of programs that helped innumerable families, and they set policies in motion that improved the standard of living for many. The welfare of children—the primary focus of maternalists—demanded government intervention on behalf of all poor mothers, they argued. If children's outcomes and their future ability to contribute to a stronger country were to be placed squarely on the shoulders of women, as they agreed it should, then it was the obligation of the state, they claimed, to ensure that mothers had the training, resources, and education necessary to fulfill their familial, and thus patriotic, duties.

In 1912, Florence Kelly and settlement house advocate Lillian Wald founded the Children's Bureau. As the first federal agency to be run primarily by women, the bureau was initially created in response to the disturbing infant (and mother) mortality rates, which the government seemed to be ignoring. These rates were especially high in poorer areas. The Children's Bureau comprised social activists and government representatives who would organize mothers' conferences that entire families would attend, run traveling clinics, distribute literature, go into the homes of families to offer training for infant and child feeding and care, and to offer instruction on home upkeep, in an effort to reduce disease and malnutrition. A multitude of mothers greatly desired and eagerly accepted the instruction that maternalists brought to them, and the collaborative efforts of all these women did in fact reduce mortality rates and promote healthier living for many families. Through time, these maternalists and pension administrators extended their purview beyond reducing mortality rates and, convinced of the superiority of methods used in middle-class white homes, pushed such methods for their own sake. The Children's Bureau's standards and methods of home and child care became the measure by which "good" mothering was judged. Women who adhered to the standards of the bureau, many of which were meticulously outlined in its widely disseminated pamphlets, such as "Infant Care" and "Child Management," earned the right to be considered worthy of government support. "Infant Care," for example, argued for methodical training such as the following:

> *The proper care of the baby consists in applying certain scientific health principles which have been reduced to working rules by specialists and made available to all mothers. . . . The care of a baby is readily reduced to a system unless he is sick. . . . The first essential in bowel training is absolute regularity. . . . The mother should observe the hour at which the baby soils his diaper. At the same hour the next day she should hold him over the chamber, using a soap stick, if necessary, to start the movement and thus continue day after day, not varying the time by five minutes, until the baby is fixed in this habit.*

The pamphlet argued that pacifiers and sucking fingers or thumbs were "disgusting" and "disfiguring to the baby's appearance." It also argued that "teaching the child to take food at regular hours and to be satisfied when fed only at these periods is the first important lesson the mother can impart. . . . This early habit of 'taking food by the clock' is most important because the health of the baby and the comfort of the mother depend so largely upon it." The bureau taught mothers to refrain from physical affection to avoid spoiling and to avoid feeding children spicy or garlicky foods such as spaghetti and goulash. Bureau standards also outlined particular methods of home upkeep, marital status, morality, and the expectation that women would not work outside the home.

The Children's Bureau and later white maternalist activist efforts were also bolstered by white concerns that another problem emerging from some families was that their methods of family life were not producing appropriate male citizens. In particular, there were concerns that immigrant and black draftees into World War I were not appropriately masculine or American enough to effectively and loyally serve their patriotic duty or to reintegrate into society after the war. Since citizens were produced in the home, maternalists contended, and therefore by mothers, government would directly benefit from addressing the presumed deficiencies of nonwhite family life and the activity of mothers in particular.

The work of maternalist reformers certainly marginalized mothering practices and beliefs that were not white and middle class. They denigrated cultural variation, thus serving racist ends. Yet their work also uprooted deep racist ideologies that assumed a biologically given "lesser race" status for immigrants and people of color and that sanctioned their subhuman treatment in many ways. Maternalists effectively lobbied for government recognition of immigrant and poor nonwhite women as contributing and voting citizens who were therefore entitled to federal and state assistance. The price of such recognition and assistance was assimilation to dominant white culture. Poor nonwhite and immigrant women were firmly instructed to live like white people in many ways and to relinquish many of their cultural practices, such as using ritual and herbal remedies in healing and birthing, using midwives, preparing the foods common to their communities but unfamiliar to white communities, and having family members living in the household beyond the nuclear group. Because poverty itself was not addressed as a social issue worthy of active reconfiguration by government, "bad mothering" was pegged as the source of the problems of the poor, rather than economics, social inequity, or preferential public policy.

Unlike black clubwomen reformers, white maternalists remained grounded in the assumption that children's and the nation's best interests are served when mothers are at home full time. This meant that they argued for important initiatives such as mothers' pensions. This financial compensation provided income for poor widowed women for their at-home mothering work, which prevented many of them from losing custody of their children because they were unable to support them. Mothers' pensions would ideally make paid employment outside the home unnecessary and would enable mothers to cultivate the kind of time-consuming motherhood understood to be necessary for children's well-being. The assumptions that were the foundation for mother's pensions also fed a distrust of institutionalized childcare and day nurseries, which might facilitate mothers' employment outside the home. Maternalists' commitment to childcare reform, therefore, was stilted. They did establish the National Federation of Day Nurseries in 1898, which provided critical resources that kept distressed families together. But institutional childcare was considered a temporary solution to a problem that was more appropriately addressed by having a wage-earning male in the family. Maternalists focused on initiatives and policies that would keep women home, such as increasing male wages so that only one employed spouse was needed per family (known as providing a "family wage"). They chose this focus rather than supporting policies such as providing childcare, reasonable wages, and improved working conditions for women, which might make mothering, working outside the home, and making purposeful choices about the men in their lives a more tenable negotiation for working-class and poor women.

Body Talk and Activism at the Turn of the Century

In the 1800s, little was said about family planning. What arguments emerged in favor of it did so later in the century and gained momentum in the early 1900s. Under the very Anglo principle of "coverture," women legally owed not only domestic service to their husbands, but also sexual and reproductive service. Such service was to be provided "on demand." And while many marital relationships were no doubt grounded in tender affection and genuine caring, neither was necessary or widely expected if husbands wanted sexual relations with their wives. In the 1870s, a movement began in Britain that called for "voluntary motherhood." Later in the United States, this notion would be used to support contraception, but at this point in the 19th century, it was used to advocate for a woman's right to limit her pregnancies by refusing her husband's sexual demands. This movement met with only moderate success given how it conflicted with widely shared assumptions about women's sexuality, especially that of white women. Because women were charged with subduing men's natural tendencies, and because women were understood to be greatly motivated by their natural moral superiority, it was assumed that they were comparatively asexual. It is true that they were expected to provide sex when their husbands wanted it, but this was framed as a kind of disinterested willingness that helped center the men and better equip them to handle the chaotic world beyond the home. Sex was a moral responsibility for women, not something that was a driving force or desire for them. So to encourage women to actively choose when they did or did not want to have sex and to make those wishes known rubbed against many people's sense of women's sexuality. For them to pointedly address sex at all seemed over the top.

Contraception, then, was no more a respectable topic of conversation or advocacy among white women than sex was in general; both were connected to excess. To talk about contraception was to talk about sex, and this was taboo in the Victorian era. In 1872, the Comstock law codified this moratorium on talk about reproduction and contraception, calling such talk or any related informational material "obscene" and making it illegal for doctors to acquire contraceptive devices that they might then sell to their patients.

Some evidence indicates that in the 1800s various groups of women, especially those who were not white and middle class, defied the law and employed their own cultural practices of birth control, as noted, for example, in Chapter 1 among enslaved women. Contraceptive and abortive practices, though, seem to have been more widely used in the early 1900s. Comstock laws held sway for some time and had extensive influence on public perception of (especially white) women's bodies, sex knowledge, sexual activity, and pregnancy prevention. In contrast, Native women, as Barbara Alice Mann points out, retained full right to sexual conduct, to making open choices about their sexual partners, and to taking contraceptive measures to determine for themselves when they would mother and how many children they would have. They practiced contraception, abortion, and infanticide in accordance with what was best for their families and communities. Their reproductive autonomy, however, was targeted by white government and healthcare institutions. Beginning in the early 1900s Native women were sterilized against their will, and their cultural reproductive and contraceptive practices were stigmatized. Loss of their reproductive agency amid greatly weakened political and economic power posed terrible and genocidal threats to Native communities.

The Comstock laws and Theodore Roosevelt's 1906 accusations of "race suicide" and critique of white women's "willful sterility" were not wholly successful in thwarting women's efforts to control their own bodies and the size of their families, as indicated by falling birthrates at the turn of the 20th century. Feminist activists defied both social convention and the law as they determined to help women protect their health and better afford to support their families by having some measure of control over if, how often, and when to become mothers. Anarchist Emma Goldman and birth control activists Margaret Sanger and Mary Ware Dennett were primary figures in this work.

Emma Goldman began lecturing publicly on contraception in 1900 and was arrested several times under the Comstock antiobscenity laws. A nurse and midwife to the immigrant population of the Lower East Side of New York, she became increasingly frustrated at the plight of the women there. Poor women's inability to gain access to midwives or other safe birthing assistance frequently posed a health risk—a risk that was compounded many times over by the squalid conditions in which many of them, especially those who were immigrants, had to live. In 1916, she addressed a large audience in New York on contraception. This lecture was particularly notable because it was the first time that instructions were publicly given about *how to use* contraception.

Mentored by Goldman, Margaret Sanger sought out multiple public venues for her lectures and demonstrations. In response to

A Plan for the Birth Control Movement

Margaret Sanger's insistent defiance of Comstock laws, which prohibited the distribution of birth control information, resulted in her arrest a number of times. After being arrested in 1914, she jumped bail and sailed to England. Just before she left, she wrote this letter to guide her supporters and to clarify the position of the movement.

Comrades and Friends

Every paper published should have a message for its readers. It should deliver it and be done. The Woman Rebel had for its aim the imparting of information of the prevention of conception. It was not the intention to labor on for years advocating the idea, but to give the information directly to those desired it. The March, May, July, August, September and October issues have been suppressed and confiscated by the Post Office. They have been mailed regularly to all subscribers. If you have not received your copies, it has been because the U.S. Post Office has refused to carry them to you.

My work on the nursing field for the past fourteen years has convinced me that the workers desire the knowledge of prevention of conception. My work among women of the working class proved to me sufficiently that it is they who are suffering because of the law which forbids the imparting of this information. To wait for this law to be repealed would be years and years hense. Thousands of un-wanted children may be born into the world in the meantime. Thousands of women made miserable and unhappy.

Why Should we wait?

her work, the Women's Political Association of Harlem was the first African American women's club to schedule lectures on birth control. Sanger founded the American Birth Control League in 1921, later named "Planned Parenthood," and in fact is credited with coining the phrase "birth control." Also disturbed by the toll that multiple births took on poor women's health and economic status, Sanger sought to make contraception legal. She opened the first birth control clinic in

Shall we who have heard the cries and seen the agony of dying Women respect the law which has caused their death?

Shall we watch in patience the murdering of 25000 women, who die each year in the U.S. from criminal abortion?

Shall we fold our hands and wait until a body of sleek and well fed politicians get ready to abolish the cause of such slaughter?

Shall we look upon a piece of parchment as greater than human happiness greater than human life?

Shall we let it destroy our womanhood, and hold millions of workers in bondage and slavery? Shall we who respond to the throbbing pulse of human needs concern ourselves with indictments, courts and judges, or shall we do our work first and settle with these evils later?

This law has caused the perpetuation of quackery. It has created the fake and quack who benefits by its existence.

Jail has not been my goal. There is special work to be done and I shall do it first. If jail comes after I shall call upon all to assist me. In the meantime I shall attempt to nullify the law by direct action and attend to the consequences later.

Over 100000 working men and women in the U.S. shall hear from me.

The Boston Tea Party was a defiant and revolutionary act in the eyes of the English Government, but to the American Revolutionist it was but an act of courage and justice.

Yours Fraternally
Margaret H. Sanger

1916, was arrested, and upon her release went back to distributing information, a level of persistence modeled for her by Goldman.

Sex education advocate Mary Dennett in 1915 founded the first birth control organization in the United States, the National Birth Control League. Dennett was a contemporary of Sanger's and though they were fighting similar battles they often did not agree on approach. Dennett focused more on getting information and contraceptive methods and devices freely into the hands of women; Sanger's approach to distribution centered on healthcare professionals. Dennett emphasized working with policy, and Sanger's emphasis was more radical (not surprising given her training with Goldman) and grounded in high-visibility demonstrations. Nevertheless, Goldman eventually split from Sanger's mission, on the grounds that Sanger was not radical enough. Sanger's zeal was later channeled into the eugenics movement, which focused in part on eliminating births by "unfit" mothers and reducing the population of "undesirable" groups, typically through coerced or forced sterilization; it was a movement that targeted poor people, immigrants, and people of color in devastating ways. In fact, as historian Linda Gordon has argued, the negative effects of Planned Parenthood's emphasis on small families, and its international focus on sterilization over contraception, might well have eclipsed its potentially positive feminist agenda for all women's freedom. Goldman, Sanger, Dennett, and the other birth control activists of their time made critical strides in women's reproductive autonomy, effectively breaking a cultural silence surrounding women's bodies and reproductive processes. Despite efforts to channel the outcome of their work toward racist ends, the seeds of reproductive rights they sowed would forever alter the landscape of women's lives.

On issues from abolition to settlement housing, contraception to education, and political activism to community leadership, women in the late 19th and early 20th centuries saw motherhood as a fertile source for power. During the next sixty years, activists would begin to question whether women's roles as mothers defined the extent of their power. Feminists would reconsider motherhood as women's primary source of identity and examine other sources of meaning for their lives, such as work, artistic creation, and political engagement beyond family concerns. They would also begin to look at motherhood in light of other family and social relationships, and they would embark on the long road to reconfiguring both the institution of the family and social policy in an effort to redistribute responsibilities, power, and resources in ways that would enable women's continued independence and freedom.

CHAPTER 3

FROM MOTHERING THE NATION TO RESTRUCTURING THE FAMILY

"SMOTHER LOVE," THE SECOND WORLD WAR, "permissive parenting," the "tangle of pathology," the "feminine mystique," the institution of motherhood, the Pill—the emergence and evolution of these phenomena from the 1920s through the 1970s gave rise to cultural changes that would have a significant impact on how mothers and motherhood were thought about, supported, and critiqued. Feminists of this period were contending, sometimes simultaneously, with popular views that motherhood held both the hope and the shame of the nation, critiques of motherhood as a source of women's oppression, and reconfigurations of motherhood that afforded women greater agency within and beyond it.

After the Nineteenth Amendment was ratified in 1920, giving women the right to vote, women's focus seemed to shift. Instead of working to extend their influence and status beyond the domestic sphere, many women were pursuing marriage as the primary "career" choice. New "labor-saving devices" created the impetus to develop new, more meticulous, methods of home and childcare, which in turn helped women to make sense of turning domesticity into a career. Colleges accommodated and fed this turn by offering home economics and motherhood courses. Women's magazines fed the resurgence of domestic affection in notable ways, assuring women that homemaking was the most rewarding occupation. These magazines also argued that since men were naturally self-centered and women were naturally self-sacrificing, women would experience no unrest or dissatisfaction if they could simply accept the identities coming from these biological facts.

The Good/Bad Mother Dualism in Wartime and the Postwar Years

Having begun a campaign in 1917 to standardize and nationalize policy that would protect women and children from high maternal and infant mortality rates, white maternalists saw the Sheppard-Towner Maternity and Infancy Protection Act become law in 1921, under the leadership of U.S. Children's Bureau chief Julia Lathrop. The first "women's" legislation to pass after women achieved the vote, the bill was a collaborative effort between the Children's Bureau, grassroots maternalist activists, and clubwomen. Poor women appealed to the bureau to help them in their arduous carework and to teach them how to ensure the good health of their families. The result was Sheppard-Towner, which provided states with federal matching grants to support instruction on nutrition and hygiene, visiting nurses, and prenatal and child health clinics; its focus was largely educational. The act was the product of years of effort, largely by women activists, to establish the idea of child welfare and the government's responsibility for it. For the most part, Sheppard-Towner built on the work of the Children's Bureau to promote good health and hygiene by instructing women's mothering and domestic practices, with particular attention to families in rural areas.

Feminist law and social policy researcher Gwendolyn Mink explains in *The Wages of Motherhood* that Sheppard-Towner "was women's first legislative achievement as political citizens." It was directed at maintaining a definition of womanhood that was focused on children and dependent on men or government, and a definition of good mothering that was reflective of white culture and middle-class values. It focused on education, advice, supervision, and conformity as the means to, in Lathrop's terms, "Americanize the family."

As the 1920s wore on, maternalist efforts began to diminish. NACW and black women's club efforts continued, though they were exacting a toll on its leaders. With Jim Crow laws still firmly in place, black women's efforts to rally communities were persistently thwarted because traveling the lecture and activist circuit was made taxing by continued segregation that affected eating establishments, public lodging, and transportation facilities or quarters. As most of these women were mothers themselves, it became an increasingly demanding and demoralizing task to "mother the race" and their own children too in a society that continued to treat them as second-class citizens.

As maternally motivated activism waned, attitudes about the pure intentions and outcomes of mothering and women's capacity for building a nation came under more and more scrutiny. Paradoxically, motherhood continued to be celebrated as the pinnacle of womanhood and the hope of the nation, even as public discourse generated misgivings about the kinds of people mothers were producing. For the first time, middle-class mothers became the objects of scathing critique; no mother of any race or class was spared surveillance in this era of increased focus on mothers as potentially "dangerous" for children, and for men.

At the end of the twenties, the stock market crashed, precipitating the decadelong Great Depression that shook the foundations of U.S. economy, policy, culture, and family life. The Depression pulled public attention away from issues such as gender and race equity. At the same time, it challenged deeply entrenched dominant views about whites' natural superiority and success because the Depression's economic devastation cut across race lines. It also challenged widely accepted beliefs about the relationship between masculinity and the ability to earn a family's living, yet when men could not find work, or enough of it, the microscope was frequently turned on women. Women were sharply admonished for working outside the home if they had any option not to, both because of its supposed negative consequences for children and because it "robbed" men of jobs. Mothers were watched with a piercing gaze and suspicion for the likelihood that they were responsible for producing adults who were not "well adjusted," and in particular men who were not masculine. Whether or not families could effectively survive the defeating effects of the Depression depended on how well mothers navigated their families through it; fathers and government were not likewise implicated. Mothering, therefore, was regarded with deep suspicion that it just might be the source of all that was wrong with the country.

As World War II began to pull the United States out of the economic depression, attitudes about mothering morphed again to accommodate the changing economy. Workers were needed to assist with the war effort and replace the numbers of men who left the workforce to go to war. Women's roles were reconfigured, and children's needs were rearticulated. Working women no longer dealt a blow to masculinity or femininity (no matter how dirty or strenuous a woman's job was); children were fine without their moms all day, and government felt obligated to support daycare. Government propaganda during World War II convinced women that entering the workforce was their patriotic duty and that their children were the better for it. As a result, record numbers of women, especially those in the middle class, joined the large numbers of working-class women who had always been in the workforce. Public and government discourse espoused the positions that communal care of children was healthy and normal, that having children in daycare was actually good for them, and that mothers who left their kids there while they worked all day were doing the right and natural thing. After the war, however, the rhetoric directed at mothers changed again, and children were depicted as at-risk if mothers continued to work outside the home. This shift in approach was particularly complicated for single mothers—of whom there were a great number more since many husbands were killed in war—who had to continue working to keep their families alive. A renewed idea that daycare was bad for children and a sudden interest in unsupervised kids at home became the focus. Scientific and psychological studies of the time backed up the idea that "normal" mothers should *want* to return home, and those who did—either by choice or after being fired—were doing the right and natural and psychologically healthy thing.

Also after World War II, standards for child rearing began to shift again, though mothers were under no less watchful of an eye. In 1946, Benjamin Spock introduced a book that has had the most monumental impact on child rearing of perhaps any book ever. His manual, *The Common Sense Book of Baby and Child Care,* has been outsold only by the Bible. Spock's work advocated "permissive" child rearing and assumed, at its core, that there are no problem children, only problem mothers. The formerly revered mothering style that required regimen and control in the name of "independence training" was replaced by a mothering style that required warmth, affection, and nonstop attention in the name of "self-demand." Mothers were to follow their children's lead. And those who did, without being remotely distracted by any outside interests or concerns, those who spent hours talking and thinking at a child's level, those who embraced the constant emotional work on top of the physical work of mothering, would produce happy, well-adjusted citizens. These would be citizens who were unrestrained, content in their own indulgence, and, incidentally, perfect citizens for a mass-consuming culture. In the previous century mothering was to produce adults ready to assimilate into the routinized and even grueling world of business and industry; now it was to produce adults ready to gratify their desires and look outside themselves for ways to satisfy those desires, spending money on products and services that would help them do so, thus solidifying the central role of consumerism in American life. Clearly, working-class mothers, mothers of large families, single mothers, and a host of others would fail in this labor- and time-intensive style. But since dominant culture is more invested in the middle class in general, and in its members as consumers in particular, it was middle-class mothers who bore the brunt of critique. While Spock's style was permissive for children, it was highly restrictive for mothers. Adult adjustment and the whole of psychological health were understood to be rooted in the mother-child bond.

Earlier in 1942, in the midst of World War II, journalist Philip Wylie's *Generation of Vipers* had provided additional fuel for the mother-blaming fire. In his treatise, he attacked white mothers of the middle class for producing a generation of men who were unable to

The "Special Problem" of the Working Mother

Dr. Benjamin Spock's bestseller *The Common Sense Book of Baby and Child Care* is one of the most widely read and disseminated books of all time. In its several editions it gradually acknowledged fathers' roles in the care of children, but even so it remained through the years directed at heterosexual nuclear families in which fathers worked and mothers raised children at home. It was aimed at the mother as the family member who would be available to children and responsive to their needs. This emphasis on at-home mothers and the nuclear family was particularly evident in the fact that his treatment of single mothers and working mothers appeared at the back of the 1945 edition in a section titled "Special Problems."

The Working Mother

To work or not to work? Some mothers have to work to make a living. Usually their children turn out all right, because some reasonably good arrangement is made for their care. But others grow up neglected and maladjusted. It would save money in the end if the government paid a comfortable allowance to all mothers (of young children) who would otherwise be compelled to work. You can think of it this way: useful, well-adjusted citizens are the most valuable possessions a country has,

fulfill even the most basic expectations for masculinity and citizenship. These failed men relinquished control of their income to their mothers and later to their wives; they became "neuters" and "geldings" whose relationship with their mothers led to "pitiable weakness." According to Wylie, young men's "megaloid momworship," led by mothers themselves, had stripped them of their boyhood aspirations to explore and conquer. "It is difficult to put young men in the mood for war," Wylie argued, "when they come to arms fresh from reviling arms, and in the pantywaist besides, which their moms had put upon them." Mothers were narcissistic and power hungry, Wylie claimed, and sacrificed their sons for their own vapid gains. These women and the blind worship of motherhood despite its destructive tendencies—"momism" as he titled it—were sure to tear the nation apart.

and good mother care during early childhood is the surest way to pro-
duce them. It doesn't make sense to let mothers go to work making
dresses in factories or tapping typewriters in offices, and have them pay
other people to do a poorer job of bringing up their children.

A few mothers, particularly those with professional training, feel that
they must work because they wouldn't be happy otherwise. I wouldn't
disagree if a mother felt strongly about it, provided she had an ideal
arrangement for her children's care. After all, an unhappy mother can't
bring up very happy children.

What about the mothers who don't absolutely have to work but
would prefer to, either to supplement the family income, or because
they think they will be more satisfied themselves and therefore get
along better at home: That's harder to answer.

The important thing for a mother to realize is that the younger the
child the more necessary it is for him to have a steady, loving person
taking care of him. In most cases, the mother is the best one to give him
this feeling of "belonging," safely and surely. She doesn't quit on the job,
she doesn't turn against him, she isn't indifferent to him, she takes care
of him always in the same familiar house. If a mother realizes clearly
how vital this kind of care is to a small child, it may make it easier for
her to decide that the extra money she might earn, or the satisfaction
she might receive from an outside job is not so important after all.

The impact of Wylie's disparagements was far-reaching. Inspired by
his assaults on mothers, scholarly research, films, advice manuals, and
various pop media overflowed with depictions of deficient or menacing
mothers who were too permissive or too strict; too immersed in their
children's lives or too distant; too focused on their children's happiness
or too distracted by other interests. In the forties and fifties, men who
could not make their single wage stretch wide enough to shield their
families were assumed to be neither masculine nor responsible enough,
and again, the blame fell on mothers, who purportedly produced such
compromised citizens. Mothers were even blamed for racism. In her
bold and landmark efforts to illuminate the sources of race prejudice
in white people and to get white people to see racism as their problem,
even white, ardent antiracist Lillian Smith implicated mothers, in her

book *Killers of the Dream*, as the producers of racist attitudes. Mother blaming continued to flourish as a great American pastime.

During the fifties, images of the "traditional" nuclear family proliferated, even though such images misrepresented a majority of American families. The fifties were imagined then and are still imagined now as a time during which respectable families were self-sustaining on a single income, were sexually conservative, and were characterized by a full-time working father and a full-time at-home mother. In fact, a large majority of families were dependent on government assistance programs that funded and regulated federal housing loans and education payments and allowed a significant expansion of allowable debt. Not only was the suburban family in the 1950s more reliant on government "handouts" than any group is now, but this decade also saw the highest rates of teen pregnancy in U.S. history to date. The legendary family of the 1950s has no roots whatever in history or tradition; in fact, it stands out as an exception in U.S. history rather than the rule from which we have supposedly and regrettably since moved away. Today's rates of unmarried pregnancy, variety of family forms, women's employment, and blended families are much more similar to historical traditions begun in colonial America than are images from the fifties.

These images of white, nuclear, middle-class families proliferated largely through the explosion of consumption- and advertisement-driven television, which demanded homogenizing depictions that would appeal (and most important, sell products) to those with expendable income and that would link patriotism, consumption, and family togetherness. White middle-class women as a whole began to focus again on children, domesticity, and community and returned home, though many would repopulate the workforce once their children were older. Black middle-class women were similarly focused, though many of them continued to work or try to find employment. Race relations in the United States were becoming increasingly tense, resulting in and aggravated by, among other problems, restricted workforce access for black men; black women were especially in need of employment as a result. This spike in racial tension would lay the

The 1950s family exists in the popular American imagination as an idealized unit in which the father supported the family financially and the mother stayed at home and tended to the physical and emotional needs of her children.

foundation for the civil rights movement that followed in the next decade. Working-class white women and women of color continued to comb the workforce for jobs, but postwar perspectives about women workers complicated their efforts. Even the most skilled female workers were underpaid and placed in marginal and temporary jobs. It was largely assumed that a woman's participation in the labor pool was merely supplemental to her husband's (whether or not she actually had one, and whether or not he made a living wage or found work at all), was intermittent between children, and was more about having "pin money" than about subsistence. These assumptions served to justify women's perpetually subordinate status, their inferior treatment, and their lower pay. Such relegation was quite difficult for women who had become used to receiving respect and reasonable pay at work during the war. Moreover, many women had gotten a taste of having workplace status and had developed career aspirations and areas of expertise that were subsequently thwarted. To justify both middle-class women's return to the home and to fuel their consumption of advertised goods, domestic work and childcare became not only more labor intensive than previously, but they were also portrayed by advertisements and other media images as deeply meaningful in their own right and a sufficient source for women's entire identity and sense of value.

Work, Motherwork, and Women's Power in the Sixties

For many women in the fifties, family life offered a retreat from both the "Red Scare" of Communist influence purportedly posed by the Soviet Union and the limited job opportunities available to them no matter their levels of education. Even though women attended college in record numbers during the fifties, few of them went on for postgraduate degrees compared to those who did so in the 1920s and 1930s. At this time, most women—both white women and women of color—had jobs, not careers, and rarely could find work outside of teaching, nursing, or secretarial work; black women were, once again, employed primarily in domestic or service work. These activities were not much different from the kinds of work women did in the home and with their families, and a majority of women thought of marriage and motherhood as their primary focus.

By the sixties, mothers were faced with having to make sense of the widespread but sharply conflicting advice from "experts." On one hand, even though working-class women and middle-class black women had to work, and many other women entered the workforce by choice, experts such as the much-revered Dr. Spock still fervently argued, consistent with white maternalists earlier in the century, that full-time work and motherhood were incompatible and that children needed the constant attentions of their mothers. Conversely, experts from psychology and those influenced by Philip Wylie's *Generation of Vipers* were ominously warning about the ill effects of "smother love." At the same time, new discussion began to uproot the idea that mothers were the only appropriate caregivers for their children and challenged the belief that working moms were hazardous to their children's health;

some research even began to suggest that mothers' work outside the home had positive effects on their children. Just as attitudes about women and work had shifted during World War II, in the sixties as more women entered the workforce (by 1960, nearly one-third of women workers were mothers of children under eighteen), attitudes about what was good and right for children began to shift again. During the war women's increased workforce participation was seen as an absolute necessity, and theories of children's needs changed to accommodate that. In the sixties women's increased workforce participation was viewed by politicians, mental health professionals, and many businesses not so much as absolutely necessary but rather as absolutely inevitable, given the changing views of women's roles and rights and an increased focus on advertising, consumerism, and improving standards of living that necessitated higher incomes. Theories of childhood again changed in response to these shifts. Even the famed "Infant Care" pamphlet put out by the Children's Bureau changed its 1963 version to include references to the fathers' role in children's well-being, indicating some movement away from focusing solely on mothers as caregivers.

In 1963, feminist journalist Betty Friedan served as a voice for white middle-class mothers and their dissatisfaction with having motherhood and marriage define their personhood. Her book, *The Feminine Mystique,* generated a swell of discussion and activism about women's right to seek contentment in sources other than homemaking and child rearing. When white housewives and mothers heard other housewives and mothers admitting to a restlessness and unease about the lives they were leading, they began to turn to each other, rather than to experts and religious leaders, for information and insight about how to live more fulfilling lives. A primary answer to their malaise, Friedan and others argued, was to get out of the house and into the workforce, where they could begin to realize a new potential for themselves. And indeed, many women did so. Their increased participation in employed work began to ready the ground for changes in workplace policy that outlawed wage discrimination and gender-biased hiring practices. The Equal Employment Opportunity Commission (EEOC) was formed in

1965 to enforce the Civil Rights Act, but its commitment to policing sex discrimination was weak. Feminists lobbied for an addition to Title VII of the Civil Rights Act of 1964 that would prohibit sex discrimination in employment in addition to its protections against employment discrimination on the basis of race, creed, and national origin.

In 1966, black law professor Pauli Murray joined with Friedan, who later joined with former EEO commissioners Aileen Hernandez and Richard Graham, among others, to found the National Organization for Women (NOW), which focused primarily on equal employment opportunities. NOW also argued for fair and equitable division of labor between women and men at home, and for women's and men's shared responsibility for earning an income and caring for children. As such, it had great appeal for white, married, middle-class women, though several women of color were NOW members from the outset, including Murray, Hernandez, and politicians and civil and women's rights advocates Shirley Chisholm and Anna Arnold Hedgeman. The organization has worked, especially as it has evolved, to secure equal rights for women across race, class, sexuality, and age distinctions.

Working-class women, a large number of black women, and many other women of color had already been firmly entrenched in the workforce, in jobs that not only offered minimal pay but also minimal satisfaction. So Friedan's arguments, the work of NOW, and much of the feminist movement of the time did little for them and spoke little to the realities of their lives. In fact, the world of home and motherhood that white middle-class feminists critiqued was the very world that many working-class women and women of color longed for, and to which many of them wanted to retreat from their unfulfilling world of work. Black women in particular, who often found work only in domestic service no matter their education level, considered the opportunity to spend time caring for their *own* children and their *own* homes a privilege rather than burden.

Feeling unrepresented by not only the women's movement but also by the civil rights movement, which focused largely on the interests of black men, black women organized to ensure that their own needs and interests were addressed. They became major players and comprised the largest membership in the National Welfare Rights Organization (NWRO), founded in 1967, and they created the National Black Feminist Organization (NBFO) in 1973. A primary contribution of these groups to social justice, due in large part to black women's leadership in them, was their blend of race and class issues with gender issues. To focus on gender and class among black people was for them, as it was for clubwomen in the late 1800s and early 1900s, to strengthen the race as a whole. They worked to improve black women's wages, increase their access to education and job training, demand rights to medical care for them and their children, and resist sterilization abuses. In the late 1960s, domestic worker and civil rights activist Dorothy Bolden, who felt distanced from mainstream feminism partly because she thought it underemphasized homemaking and motherhood, organized a movement on behalf of employed black women who worked as maids, teaching them that a decent wage was essential to family well-being and rallying them to demand pay of $15 a day or walk off the job. In a similar vein, human rights advocate and feminist Johnnie Tillmon, who later became executive director of the NWRO, organized fellow welfare-receiving mothers, helping them to see how they could have more control over their lives and make a difference for themselves and others beyond home and child care. They were challenged in 1968 when Senator Russell Long referred to women welfare rights activists as "brood mares" and would not allow them to testify before the Senate Finance Committee. The NWRO responded with a summerlong campaign that began on Mother's Day that same year. Defiantly dubbed a "brood mare stampede" by Tillmon, the campaign was supported by welfare recipients across the country who marched with their children, picketed welfare centers, and protested in front of congressmen's homes.

The NWRO was reacting in part to the crippling amendments to the Social Security Act initiated the year before. Some of these changes granted authority to caseworkers to restrict a recipient's spending if

Quieting shouts of "sock it to him" from partisans in the audience, Beulah Sanders of the National Welfare Rights Organization waits to tell members of the Democratic Platform Committee that they should back a radical overhaul of the nation's welfare system at the 1968 Democratic National Convention in Chicago.

they disagreed with how the recipient managed her money or suspected she was receiving other forms of support. Recipients complained that caseworkers would go through their closets and refrigerators, look under their beds for men, and interrogate them about their purchases. NWRO members also resisted the threats to their dignity imposed by the ways in which their spending on essentials such as electricity, gas, water, and food was monitored and regulated, and the threats to survival imposed by the fact that government allocations for each of these did not cover the amounts they were paying. NWRO members lobbied for the right of poor single mothers to manage their government assistance money according to their convictions about what was best for their families, rather than be forced, for example, to use food stamps instead of than cash allotments at the grocery store. Food stamps, they argued, were not only stigmatizing for poor families and restrictive in terms of what foods could be purchased, but they also could not be used to buy other necessities such as feminine hygiene products, toilet paper, or laundry and cleaning supplies. NWRO also highlighted the connection between dignity and work. In particular, it protested against government assistance programs that required employment, on the grounds that the best work many of its members could get was in unskilled, undercompensated labor in dead-end jobs that rarely produced enough income to cover childcare and transportation and that offered no potential for a better life.

Perhaps the greatest impetus in this era for black women's advocacy efforts was the Moynihan Report of 1965. Written by Daniel Patrick Moynihan, the future senator's report set out to identify the obstacles to race progress for black communities in the United States. It argued that, while slavery and other forms of racism had thus far impeded black people from realizing their full potential, what was now and would continue to shackle black society—the primary source of black weakness—was the self-perpetuating deterioration of the black family. More important, the report claimed that a black matriarchy was at the core of this "tangle of pathology." It argued that black women, and especially their place of authority in their families, were at fault for race inequities. The cure, according to the report, was for women to step into subservient roles relative to the men's and afford men their "natural" power in the family. Many members of the black nationalist movement embraced this position, arguing that black women were to support men and produce and raise warriors for the black revolution. The National Council of Negro Women (NCNW), led by Dorothy Height, never spoke out against the report, instead agreeing that black women's focus ought to be the uplift of black men. But others reacted vociferously against it. Activists such as Jean Carey Bond and Patricia Peery, for example, wrote in their 1969 article "Has the Black Man Been Castrated?" that the idea that black "matriarchy" was figuratively "castrating" black men was a crippling myth that black communities, and women in particular, must fight against. Lifelong peace activist, writer, and black feminist Frances Beal, who was a vibrant member of the Student Nonviolent Coordinating Committee (SNCC), argued that

"Welfare as a Women's Issue"

The welfare rights movement largely comprised poor black women. They differed from mainstream feminists of the time in the value they placed on their roles as mothers and on their right to care for them and their homes. They also differed in their resistance to the idea that paid employment would liberate them, since the work they were able to secure typically was not fulfilling and did not provide sufficient wages. Johnnie Tillmon, who became executive director of the National Welfare Rights Organization in 1972, nonetheless saw poor women's rights as a central element of the women's liberation movement. In this piece, written in 1972 for *Ms.* magazine, she explains why.

Welfare's like a traffic accident. It can happen to anybody, but especially it happens to women.

And that is why welfare is a women's issue. For a lot of middle-class women in this country, Women's Liberation is a matter of concern. For women on welfare it's a matter of survival. . . .

The truth is that A.F.D.C. [Aid to Families with Dependent Children] is like a supersexist marriage. You trade in a man for the man. But you can't divorce him if he treats you bad. He can divorce you, of course, cut you off anytime he wants. But in that case, he keeps the kids, not you.

The man runs everything. In ordinary marriage, sex is supposed to be for your husband. On A.F.D.C., you're not supposed to have any sex at all. You give up control of your own body. It's a condition of aid. You may even have to agree to get your tubes tied so you can never have more children just to avoid being off welfare.

The man, the welfare system, controls your money. He tells you what to buy, what not to buy, where to buy it, and how much things cost. If things—rent, for instance—really cost more than he says they do, it's just too bad for you. . . .

The President keeps repeating the "dignity of work" idea. What dignity? Wages are the measure of dignity that society puts on a job. Wages and nothing else. There is no dignity in starvation. Nobody denies, least of all poor women, that there is dignity and satisfaction in being able to support your kids through honest labor.

We wish we could do it.

The problem is that our country's economic policies deny the dignity and satisfaction of self-sufficiency to millions of people—the millions who suffer everyday in underpaid dirty jobs—and still don't have enough to survive.

People still believe that old lie that A.F.D.C. mothers keep on having kids just to get a bigger welfare check. On the average, another baby means another $35 a month—barely enough for food and clothing. Having babies for profit is a lie that only men could make up, and only men could believe. Men, who never have to bear the babies or have to raise them and maybe send them to war.

There are a lot of other lies that male society tells about welfare mothers; that A.F.D.C. mothers are immoral, that A.F.D.C. mothers are lazy, misuse their welfare checks, spend it all on booze and are stupid and incompetent. . . .

If I were president, I would solve this so-called welfare crisis in a minute and go a long way toward liberating every woman. I'd just issue a proclamation that "women's" work is real work.

In other words, I'd start paying women a living wage for doing the work we are already doing—child-raising and house-keeping. And the welfare crisis would be over, just like that. Housewives would be getting wages, too—a legally determined percentage of their husband's salary—instead of having to ask for and account for money they've already earned.

For me, Women's Liberation is simple. No woman in this country can feel dignified, no woman can be liberated, until all women get off their knees. That's what N.W.R.O. is all about—women standing together, on their feet.

having and raising children is *not* black women's most productive role. She asserted, as did Michele Wallace in her later book *Black Macho and the Myth of the Super-Woman,* that for black women to be subservient to men and to focus on keeping up their houses and building up their men was counterrevolutionary. Black women's response to both the Moynihan Report and to those who supported its claims amplified discussions of motherhood and its political implications that would have far-reaching impact in the next decade.

Black social worker and activist Patricia Robinson, along with writers such as Angela Davis and Alice Walker, elaborated discussions of the black mother and her ties to social power and resistance. They spelled out a pro-mother stance that would serve as foundational for the feminist considerations of motherhood that would find force in the midseventies. Robinson, whose arguments were in synch with the essentializing arguments of cultural feminism that were beginning to unfold, saw the first mother, the earth itself, and the Madonna as black, and she drew links between the oppression of women, blacks, and nature that would feed later ecofeminist thought. In a related but different vein, in 1971 Angela Davis wrote an article, "Reflections on the Black Woman's Role in the Community of Slaves," from the Marin County Jail, where she was held on charges stemming from her radical political activism. In it, she redefined the notion of black "matriarchy" to highlight how black mothers regularly performed powerful acts of resistance to the institution of slavery within their enslaved families and that such strength was part of the enduring legacy of black people and should be venerated. Robinson linked the black woman's procreative body to larger systems of human community, and Davis linked black women's maternal labor to revolutionary cultural change. Walker's work extolled the symbolic and mythological qualities of the black mother-daughter relationship and illustrated how current black women could draw sustainable strength through connection with the mother. Activist and writer Cherríe Moraga would, in the 1980s, continue to explore this theme as she wrestled through the tensions between breaking from the cultural and heterosexual positions of her mother, Moraga's own identity as a Chicana lesbian, and her need to connect with her mother as both a woman and a person of color.

Changing the Family in the Seventies

By the 1970s, the idea that women should have opportunities that extended beyond motherhood and the home was established and embraced by many. Women were entering formerly all-male occupations, and black middle-class women entered the "white collar" work that matched their educations. Even so, feminist writing and activism still was largely centered on shaping public thought and personal perceptions about why such extension of women's identities was important, not just for women but for the broader society, and on arguing for equal power in the home, in the workplace, and in activist circles. Three popular anthologies offered a representation of related feminist work published at the time. Robin Morgan's 1970 collection, *Sisterhood Is Powerful,* featured essays that critiqued workplace policies and experiences; religious, academic, and other institutions, including marriage and capitalism; and the psychological and sexual repression of women. Authors in the 1970 anthology *The Black Woman,* edited by activist, community organizer, and artist Toni Cade, wrote mostly about black empowerment and struggle and posited new definitions for black womanhood. Writers such as Cade and Frances Beal took issue with many black men's ready acceptance of the idea that "matriarchy" plagued their families and, as a result, their communities. Contributors to Leslie Tanner's anthology, *Voices from Women's Liberation*, dispelled myths about women and addressed a range of topics, including connections between women, liberation for girls, radical feminism, and men's resistance to women's liberation.

While many works critiqued the institution of marriage and women's status in it, only a handful of writings in the early seventies spoke directly of motherhood. For many feminists, a focus on motherhood would counteract their efforts to reshape cultural conceptions of women as persons who are defined by their relationships with the home and children. Many believed there had been enough talk about women and the domestic realm and women weren't getting any freer; it was time to talk about something else for a change. Some feminists, though, made efforts to reshape cultural conceptions by talking about these issues in new ways. Linda Gordon's "Functions of the Family" examined multiple ways in which the family operated as a site of women's oppression and offered alternatives to thinking about social relations primarily in terms of the nuclear family. She argued that resisting women's sexual repression, recognizing that marriage resulted in ownership of women and children more than in love for them, and acknowledging the larger societal value of women's work in the home were among the necessary steps that the women's liberation movement needed to take in its effort to change women's lives. Carol Glassman's "Women and the Welfare System," Carol Driscoll's "The Abortion Problem," and Louise Gross and Phyllis MacEwan's "On Day Care" discussed links between these specific issues and mothers' secondary status. Gross and MacEwan's piece was significant in light of the loss sustained by poor women over the 1971 Child Development Act. In 1969, President Richard Nixon had declared that all children, regardless of their social, economic, or family backgrounds, had a *right* to comprehensive child development programs and that those with the greatest need would receive highest priority. Nixon further agreed that the federal government ought to be responsible for subsidizing programs such as daycare, and therefore for helping low-income mothers gain and hold on to full-time employment. Nixon reversed his position, however, when the Child Development Act of 1971 came before him, and to the surprise of mother activists and others, he vetoed it.

While NOW did not make motherhood a central element in its agenda, it did address policies that would have a direct impact on mothers and families. In addition to its concerted efforts to address workplace rights and access, NOW agitated for changes for homemakers. In 1978, NOW drafted and lobbied for the Homemaker's Bill of Rights, which demanded economic recognition for mothers and homemakers. Coining the slogan EVERY MOTHER IS A WORKING MOTHER, NOW called for "acknowledgement of unpaid mothering and caregiving work" as a critical and valuable component of the U.S. economy. The resolution argued that it is the community, family, and larger society that benefit from the homemaker's labor, much more than the woman herself; it also denounced the use of the phrase "non-working" women to refer to homemakers and argued that they should in fact receive both the recognition and the rights granted to paid workers such as social security, disability, and retirement benefits and the right to a safe workplace. NOW's efforts in this regard were preceded at an international level by those of Selma James, an American feminist and anticapitalist who organized the International Wages for Housework Campaign in 1972 in an effort to call attention to domestic and childcare work as *work*—as *labor* that ought to be financially compensated. Those who raise children, she argued, have a right to a living wage; their work is no less valuable to sustaining society than other paid employment.

Other feminists took a radical look at the links between women's oppression and family structures. Utopian feminist writer Shulamith Firestone's 1970 book *The Dialectic of Sex,* for example, suggested that the problem for women was the biological necessity of pregnancy and birth, which were, she argued, inherently oppressive, even "barbaric," and that liberation for women was contingent on the role that technology would play in freeing them from both. And British feminist Juliet Mitchell, in her 1971 book *Woman's Estate*, focused on women's economic circumstance and its role in their exploitation. She critiqued social patterns in which women's family (reproduction) work was accorded no real social value while their access to valued occupational (production) work and the right to dignified, wage-earning work were impeded. She argued too that reproduction was largely involuntary for women and that sexuality must be differentiated both from it (through, for example, readily accessible contraception) and from marriage if people were to live freely. Psychologist and feminist writer Dorothy Dinnerstein wrote in her 1976 book *The Mermaid and the Minotaur* that mother-centered childcare solidified inequalities between women and men. Some feminists later critiqued Dinnerstein for the mother-blaming flavor of her argument that current social problems had their roots in mothers' caring for children.

NOW's Homemaker's Bill of Rights

In 1978, the National Organization for Women issued the "Homemaker's Bill of Rights: Economic Recognition for Homemakers." This document made clear NOW's support of women's right to be homemakers and to have their carework valued and recognized as making economic contributions to the U.S. gross national product. It also made clear that, given such contributions, homemaking ought to offer benefits similar to other working professions.

WHEREAS, society has not recognized the economic value of the goods and services provided by the homemaker to her/his family and the community; and

WHEREAS, the lack of value has resulted not only in the evaluation of homemakers as "non-working" women, but has also deprived the homemaker of job related benefits that paid workers take for granted; and

WHEREAS, the lack of recognition of the economic value of homemaking has had an adverse impact on women in paid employment, especially in those occupations seen as an extension of a homemaker's duties, such as nursing, education, restaurant service, domestic service and office work; and

WHEREAS, the homemakers' rights committee has been charged with the duty of proposing a bill of rights for homemakers;

THEREFORE BE IT RESOLVED, that the National Organization for Women endorses the proposal of economic recognition for homemakers, as follows:

In recognition of the fact that it is not the homemaker who benefits most from her/his unpaid labor, but it is the community and family and through them all of society, homemakers should be granted the recognition and rights of paid, skilled workers:

* *through independent social security coverage in her/his own name, portable into and out of marriage and continuing as the homemaker leaves and reenters the paid workforce, containing provision for disability and retirement benefits adequate to maintain a decent standard of living;*

* *through inclusion of the value of goods and services produced and provided by homemakers in the gross national product;*

* *through revision of welfare laws so that a low-income home-maker can remain at home with her/his family, rather than be forced to take a second, paying job;*

* *through development of flexible-time and part-time employment, and the development of adequate flexible-time and part-time child care facilities to make these jobs more available to parents of young children;*

* *through civil and criminal protection from spousal rape and domestic abuse;*

* *through providing the homemaker with a safe workplace and adequate housing regardless of income;*

* *through comprehensive review of current domestic relations laws to challenge and change those laws, statutes, procedures and codes that deprive homemakers of dignity, security and recognition;*

* *through recognition of the right to retire or change jobs.*

AND BE IT FURTHER RESOLVED, that the National Organization for Women adopts the proposals of economic rights within marriage, economic rights for homemakers in transition, and economic recognition for homemakers as a comprehensive statement of a bill of rights for homemakers.

Psychoanalytic and feminist theorist and writer Nancy Chodorow sought explanations about gender differences and the tendency for women to connect with others, to nurture, and to mother that were not based in the popular biological explanations of the time. She advanced a theory in her 1978 book *The Reproduction of Mothering* that would have far-reaching impact in both psychology and feminism. Chodorow argued that children's identity, and in particular gender identity, was grounded in their relationship with their primary caregiver; she presumed that this was the mother for most children. Girls became mothers, became nurturers, rather than being born that way, because they were primarily cared for by mothers, women with whom they became *integrated* as they learned how to be female. Mothers re-created and reproduced mothering in their daughters. Boys, in contrast, who were also cared for by their mothers, learned that to be male, they must first *differentiate* from their primary caregiver mothers and become not-female. They saw themselves as separate from, rather than integrated with, others. If children were raised primarily by fathers or experienced equally shared parenting, Chodorow's work suggested, gender would shake out differently. Feminists of color disputed Chodorow's theory on the grounds that the communal rearing of children practiced in their communities did not typically produce single, primary caregivers and on the grounds that it presumed that sharing child rearing with a male partner was possible when, for many, it wasn't. Others critiqued the theory on the grounds that, in the end, it resulted in citing mothers as responsible for producing boys' and men's disconnected behavior and for directing girls' energies into mothering and away from other areas of identity development.

One of the most important distinctions in feminist maternal thought and activism has its roots in the midseventies. In 1974, sociologist Jessie Bernard's *The Future of Motherhood* began to expand the focus on oppression by critiquing motherhood as an institution. Examining the politics of "motherwork" (a phrase brought into feminist maternal studies by Bernard and popularized later by black feminist Patricia Hill Collins), Bernard critiqued the current construction of motherhood—in which women engaged in household and childcare labor but not wage-earning work or larger social involvement, and in which women displayed all of the nurturance and compassion in the family but none of the strength and power—as not only historically unique and rife with problems, but also as marked by a social isolation that was detrimental to both women and children. So far, the feminist emphasis that the early seventies offered on motherhood was on identifying the ways that women's self-determination was constricted by familial and social structures. But feminist examinations of motherhood began to expand after the midseventies. Adrienne Rich's 1976 book *Of Woman Born* distinguished between the *institution* of motherhood and *experiences* of mothering. Rich's breakthrough work allowed feminists to find a space between, on one hand, dominant culture's insistence that motherhood is the pinnacle of womanhood and femininity and that without it there is no way for women to find happiness and, on the other hand, radical feminist critiques of the time that said motherhood is inherently oppressive and there is no way to find happiness in it.

Following Rich, feminists were able to offer a more nuanced critique of how motherhood *could* function as oppressive but wasn't necessarily or inherently this way. They argued that what was oppressive was the *institution* of motherhood—the equating of womanhood with motherhood, the expectation that women should be economically dependent on men, the unequal distribution of household and social power that stemmed from that, and the limitations on women's access to gratifying work and education outside the home. Some, including Rich, poet Audre Lorde, and ecofeminist Susan Griffin, argued that the *experience* of mothering could be fulfilling and interesting, particularly if the oppressive structures of motherhood were dismantled. Lorde's essay "Man Child: A Black Lesbian Feminist's Response," first published in 1979, was particularly influential for a number of reasons. It unfolded a narrative of lesbian motherhood and it attended to the mother-son relationship, expanding feminist focus beyond straight women raising

Mother's Day Incantation

WITCH was a submovement within the late sixties and seventies women's liberation movement. Initiated in New York in 1968, the Women's International Terrorist Conspiracy from Hell pledged to revolt against oppressive policies in the United States, especially as they related to corporate America and its impact on citizens of the United States and other countries. They used radical theatrical methods to call attention to local, national, and international issues. WITCH organized in radical activist groups called "covens" all over the country and in Tokyo. Groups played with the WITCH acronym to highlight the current focus of their group, using names such as Women Infuriated at Taking Care of Hoodlums; Women Incensed at Telephone Company Harassment; Women's Independent Taxpayers, Consumers, and Homemakers; and Women Inspired to Commit Herstory. The incantation below, which critiques the institution of motherhood, was crafted by Women Interested in Toppling Consumption Holidays.

Every year we set aside
a very special day
to remind you, Martyr Dear,
that home is where you stay.

Your family wants to thank you
for your martyrdom.
After all, without you
no real work would get done.

empowered daughters. Lorde also focused a lens of intersectionality on motherhood that looked simultaneously at race, gender, and sexuality, even as it explored the identity-shaping experiences of mothering.

Like Lorde, Jane Lazarre employed candor and courage in her writing about mothering. In her 1976 book *The Mother Knot,* Lazarre considered her conflicting feelings of fierce affection for her child and frustration with mothering borne out of her equally passionate desire to write. Discussing the pull between these two forces, particularly in

While hubby challenges the world
his wonders to perform
you cook his meals, clean his home
and keep his bedside warm.

Your children are your challenge,
in them your dreams are sown.
You've given up your own life
and live for them alone.

Now look upon your daughter
will she too be enslaved
to a man, a home, and family
or can she still be saved?

This is your real challenge—
renounce your martyrdom!
Become a liberated mother
a woman, not a "mom."

light of the still widely held assumptions that, as the woman/mother, she was responsible for navigating her way through both work and parenthood (and her husband was not), Lazarre's book was part of a growing body of work that would reject the dualism of motherhood-as-sublime and motherhood-as-oppressive. Such a body of work would continue into the nineties, where it would swell and spill over into the 21st century as it seeped into online mother communities and blogs.

The Body and Reproductive Agency

Changing views of child rearing and women's workplace roles coincided with shifts in women's reproductive agency. Estelle Griswold, executive director of the Planned Parenthood League of Connecticut, was arrested in 1961 for violating a Connecticut law that prohibited the use of, or assistance in using, any information about or device for contraception. The court case that resulted legalized the use of contraception among married couples and officially overturned the Comstock laws that had been in place for a century. The 1965 *Griswold v. Connecticut* decision sparked changes in women's reproductive control that would affect family size as well as work and educational opportunities. It also contributed to the momentum of the new decade's feminism.

Although the Pill was approved by the FDA in 1960, Comstock laws still in place restricted women's access to it. The 1965 ruling in *Griswold v. Connecticut* began to open avenues for its use as a

Estelle Griswold and Cornelia Jahncke of the Planned Parenthood League of Connecticut celebrate the U.S. Supreme Court decision in Griswold v. Connecticut, *which protected the right of married women to practice contraception.*

contraceptive, though the ruling legalized use only for married women. It would take continued activist efforts through the sixties and later to broaden access to the Pill to single and young women. Inspired by these changes, women began to go public with discussions of sex and reproduction. Such discussions were further fed by women's involvement in "consciousness raising" (CR) groups, which had their roots in the 1960s women's liberation movement. Begun by white women, these informal, community-based groups provided a place where participants openly and honestly confronted questions about power in their lives and drew from each other's experiences and narratives as sources of strength and knowledge. In CR groups, women discovered the ways that "the personal is political"—in other words, that the frustrations and ambivalence they felt about their lives had their roots in larger social issues—and that those issues could be addressed through social action. Although women of color tended not to use the CR label because of its affiliation with white feminists and their tendency to avoid issues of race and class, they did organize similar groups in which they discussed personal issues and their political or power-related implications, seeking to have their "consciousness raised" by the insights and experiences of other women. Issues related to the body, sexuality, and reproductive health were an important part of CR discussions. In some of them, women learned to shed their inhibitions and shame about their bodies by teaching each other, for example, how to insert a speculum and see what their own vaginas looked like, rather than relinquish all control of that knowledge to their doctors.

This emphasis on women demystifying their bodies and learning to look at (and into) them and to ask questions so they could better understand them received an even wider distribution through the publication of a groundbreaking book. In 1970, the Boston Women's Health Book Collective released a newsprint booklet, *Women and Their Bodies*. It was widely distributed and read—"an underground success," according to the collective. The book was professionally published in 1973 as *Our Bodies, Ourselves*. As a critical part of the women's health movement in the United States, this book was characterized by its bold appeal to women to take charge of their own reproductive lives by understanding their own bodies and by making purposeful choices about contraception, pregnancy, and childbirth. This appeal, and women's widespread willingness to answer it, represented a profound shift in health care for women. They began to take the lead in their own reproductive health rather than rely on primarily male doctors for their "expert" advice. *Our Bodies, Ourselves* provided the information, diagrams, photographs, and frank treatment of taboo topics that helped them do it. The book did and still does stir a good bit of controversy. (It is in fact still banned from some high school and public libraries around the country.) It has seen multiple adaptations and several different languages and its various versions are still in publication. In 1977, the Boston Women's Health Book Collective self-published *Nuestros Cuerpos*, the Spanish translation of the book. The 1978 edition of *Our Bodies, Ourselves* was revised to include sections that assured women that they could certainly be complete human beings without ever having children at all. Such an audacious suggestion, along with other radical questioning of the widely held assumptions about the role of reproduction in women's lives, was often misread, from outside of feminism and later even by feminists themselves, as an "attack" on mothers and families.

The 1973 Supreme Court ruling in *Roe v. Wade* guaranteed women the right to reproductive control through access to abortion. The decision, grounded in the protection of a woman's right to privacy, was the result of a lawsuit filed on behalf of Norma McCorvey ("Jane Roe") against Texas district attorney Henry B. Wade; it was argued by attorneys Sarah Weddington and Linda Coffee. The *Roe v. Wade* decision was a victory for feminist activists and for women nationwide. It was short-lived, however, for poor women. Initially, they had access to abortion because its costs were covered under Medicaid benefits. But in 1976, the passage of the Hyde Amendment restricted Medicaid so that it excluded abortion coverage, and this meant the end of access to abortions for poor women.

Even though large numbers of feminists rallied behind an abortion rights agenda, others, many of whom were women of color, broke affiliations with them. Because women of color and poor women were criticized for their family size in ways that other women weren't, many of them preferred to channel their reproductive rights efforts into being able to *have* and to *support* their children, rather than to restrict their births. Political activist and author Angela Davis explained in her book *Women, Race, and Class*, for example, that many black and Hispanic women did not identify with the movement to legalize abortion; they did not view pregnancy or motherhood in terms of oppression but rather as significant acts that are particularly heavy with meaning for marginalized women, who are routinely denied meaningful opportunities. Moreover, some black women allied with black nationalists who held that limiting births through abortion, and even through contraception, were strategies that could be used by white power structures to diminish and weaken the race.

Women of color of various classes also were confronting other restrictions on their reproductive control. Within the dominant culture, the poorer among them were fighting against coerced and forced sterilization as a means of limiting family size. Within their own communities, they were told that they were responsible for strengthening the movement by increasing their population. Activists Frances Beal, Toni Cade, the Black Women's Liberation Group (BWLG), and the black feminist group Combahee River Collective, among others, responded to both sides of this argument. Beal called sterilization abuse "outright surgical genocide," while Cade and the BWLG urged women to decide for themselves whether and when to have children, how many they wanted, and how far apart to have them. Cade argued that the Pill was merely a step toward, and not the answer to, women's liberation, but that "dumping the pill" was not the answer to the black revolution either. These women urged other black women to relinquish reproductive right, responsibility, and power to no one, either within or outside their communities. In 1970, Mexican American activist and feminist Jennie Chavez organized La Chicana women's group on her University of New Mexico campus. In an article

A Revolution Within a Revolution Has Begun

In her 1972 article, "A New Revolution Within a Revolution Has Begun," written for *Mademoiselle* magazine, La Chicana women's group founder Jennie Chavez argued for coalition building among Mexican American women. She worked to break through the stereotype that Mexican American women have to choose between loyalty to their ethnic community and loyalty to communities of powerful women.

As the women's liberation movement is becoming stronger, there is another women's movement that is effecting change in the American revolution of the 1970s—the Mexican-American women, las Chicanas, las mujeres. . . .

As Chicanas, discriminated against not only by the white dominant society, but also by our own men who have been adhering to the misinterpreted tradition of machismo, we cannot isolate ourselves from them for a simple (or complex) reason. We must rely on each other to fight the injustices of the society which is oppressing our entire ethnic group. . . .

[I have been] called a white woman for organizing a Las Chicanas group on the University of New Mexico campus. I was not only ostracized by men but by women. Some felt I would be dividing the existing Chicano group on campus (the United Mexican-American Students, UMAS), some were simply afraid of displeasing the men, some felt that I was wrong and my ideas "white" and still others felt that their contribution to La Causa of El Movimiento was in giving the men moral support from the kitchen. . . .

Chicanas, traditionally, have been tortilla-makers, baby-producers, to be touched but not heard. As the social revolution for all people's freedoms has progressed, so Chicanas have caught the essence of freedom in the air. The change occurred slowly. Mexican-American women have been reluctant to speak up, afraid they might show up the men in front of the white man—afraid that they may think our men not men. Now, however, the Chicana is becoming as well-educated and as aware of oppression, if not more so, as the Mexican-American male. The women are now ready to activate themselves. They can no longer remain quiet and a new revolution within a revolution has begun. . . . Women, as women's lib advocates know, are capable of great physical endurance so it has been with women of our ethnic group. In order to someday obtain those middle-class goods (which in my eyes oppress more people than they liberate from "drudgery") our women have not only been working at slave jobs for the white society as housemaids, hotel maids, and laundry workers, but have tended also to the wants of a husband and many children—many children because contraceptives have been contrary to the ethnic idea of La Familia (with all its socio-political-economic implications). The new breed of Chicanas are changing their puritanical mode of dress, entering the professions of law, business, medicine, and engineering. They are no longer afraid to show their intellect, their capabilities and their potential. More and more they oppose the Catholic Church, to which a large majority of our ethnic group belongs, challenging its sexual taboos as well as the idea that all Catholic mothers must be baby-producing factories and that contraceptives are a sin.

As the new breed of Mexican-American women we have been, and probably will continue to be, ridiculed by our men for attempting the acrobatics of equity. We may well be ostracized by La Familia for being vendidos, sellouts to the "white ideas" of late marriage, postponing or not wanting children and desiring a vocation other than tortilla-rolling, but I believe that this new breed of bronze womanhood, as all women today, will be a vanguard for world change.

in *Mademoiselle* magazine, written in 1972, Chavez worked to create stronger feminist alliances among Mexican American women. Her efforts resisted the cultural pressure imposed on Mexican American women to have multiple children and to seek no vocation beyond the home. She argued against the dualistic thinking that restricted women of color, asserting that they could resist both racist power coming from outside their communities and sexist power coming from within it, and that they could be both self-determined *and* integral to La Familia at the same time.

Feminist activism and writing during the sixties and seventies reshaped the landscape of family, work, and reproductive choices— for all women, including mothers. The coming decades would both solidify these changes and bring a backlash against them. For mothers, this would mean an expansion of what counted as "family," an invigorated exploration of mother identity, and a concentrated analysis of motherhood and class. It also would mean confronting a forceful and reactionary conservatism that would work to narrow the definition of family and the government's role in supporting it, restrict women's maternal self-determination, and revisit Victorian ideas of sentimental motherhood.

CHAPTER 4

FROM PRONATALISM TO MOMMY BLOGS

FAMILY VALUES, "POSTFEMINISM," OPERATION RESCUE, backlash, the Mommy Wars, and the "memoirs"—in the late 20th and early 21st centuries feminists faced a series of conservative efforts to reduce all of womanhood to motherhood (even as these efforts impeded possibilities for mothers to care for their children in truly self-determined ways), and they fought to determine the shape that motherhood should take for different women. This period was also marked both by contested views of families and work and by contested views of women's bodies, as illustrated in enduring debates over innate maternal qualities, reproductive control, and the idea of a universal experience of motherhood. Feminists continued to confront the mythical "split" between public and private by highlighting the ways, in particular, that the policies, perceptions, and institutions of public life affected the experience, conditions, and possibilities for private life. In the 1980s, often touted as one of the most affluent periods in the United States, lay the roots of heightened class tensions and a renewed conservative political stronghold that would work to narrow who gets to count as a family, what qualifies as "good" mothering, and who is entitled to make decisions and demands about at-home or at-work labor. Feminists worked to expose those roots and to cultivate conditions in which women's self-determination—maternal or otherwise—could flourish.

The Anti-Mother Myth

In contrast to earlier periods, countless and diverse women have been writing about and advocating on behalf of mothers in the period from the 1980s to today. Through time, feminists and other women in the United States have come to talk about motherhood, mothering, and reproduction in their own right. Their willingness to speak directly to such concerns has often been misread. Many people have believed that feminism as a whole has taken a stand *against* mothering and families. Antifeminists of the seventies such as Phyllis Schlafly, religious leaders such as Jerry Falwell, and talk radio hosts such as Rush Limbaugh and Laura Schlessinger have claimed that the goal of feminism is to undermine mothering and the family. What feminists have actually tried to undermine is a notion of family that requires a breadwinning, decision-making father and a nurturing, submissive at-home mother. And they have brought to this effort multiple, varied, and sometimes conflicting perspectives that cannot be reduced to a single goal.

The breadth of writing and activism that characterizes U.S. feminism has certainly debunked the mythical idea that feminists are anti-mother. Feminists, especially since the 1960s, have advocated for broadened and more equitable opportunities for women, including mothers, and they have pointed out how dominant views of what is best for children are class and race biased. They have argued that women should have the power to decide when and how often they have children or whether even to have them at all, and they have critiqued the idea that only a wife, husband, and children together constitute a family. Feminists have asserted that our social institutions (such as education, healthcare, media, government, capitalism) take as their starting point the secondary status of women, and they've identified ways that this status is grounded in how we have chosen to define and structure "the family." The positions they have taken are profoundly more complex than "mother-hating."

Feminists have certainly had much to say about how motherhood is constructed, who tends to have what kinds of power in different families, and what opportunities for self-development are opened up or closed off by the activities of mothering. They have critiqued the United States' "pronatalism"—the excessive and sometimes obsessive focus on babies and children that often obscures the impact that raising, educating, and caring for children has on families, institutions, and individuals. Such infatuation with babies is often celebrated at the expense of women's self-determination, of children who are no longer babies, and of individual and family economic stability. Feminists have advocated for changes in how "the family" is defined and government's and religion's roles in shaping family experiences. They have argued for different social arrangements that would redistribute responsibilities of home, children, and community more equitably. And they certainly have noted that current social arrangements, including how we view motherhood, work against women in many ways and could be rethought and rearranged. Some feminists have even taken the position that there is no way in a patriarchal society for motherhood to offer the possibility of freedom for women, so they argue that women should refuse to have or raise children. All of these questions and critiques have begged for a revision of motherhood as we know it. Additionally, feminism has acknowledged that many women have no interest in ever being mothers and has defended their right to that self-determination. But it has not built its arguments on a foundation of being antifamily or anti-mother.

Feminist work from the 1960s to the mid-1970s offered different possibilities for thinking about motherhood and had the courage to view it with something other than sentimentality. Feminists from the midseventies to the eighties were able to reconsider the possibility of motherhood as a site of great potential constraint and compromise for women and to examine such perspectives against their considerations of it as potentially affirming and fulfilling. Since the eighties, the United States has seen a return, in some ways, to sentimental motherhood and pronatalism. But this return has been countered by women's firmer footing in the workplace and professions, changing gender roles that have pushed more men into sharing household labor and carework, wider availability of and access to birth control, and a proliferation of women's online and print writings that honor mothering activity and admit women's ambivalence about it. Feminists have had the courage to question the sanctification of motherhood, and this has allowed them to continue reworking it so that it can benefit more women and more families in more ways.

Spotlight on the Family in the Eighties
Pronatalism, Diversionary Tactics, and Backlash

After the assiduous and engaged movement of the sixties and seventies to address social change and responsibility, and personal and governmental roles in both, the eighties took on a comparatively staid turn. Relative to earlier socially progressive developments, the 1980s were marked by regressive gender and family policies that were motivated and orchestrated by the two-term presidency of Ronald Reagan. The strategies and programs employed under "Reaganism" were the result of pointed efforts to restrict government benefits and assistance, such as aid to poor families and subsidized childcare, based on Reagan's belief that the government should not be in the business of supporting individuals. Firm believers that a free market economy would, if unimpeded by government, create the fairest society, in which those who are motivated to succeed will do so, the Reagan administration greatly reconfigured perspectives on the family and social equity. Families were the cornerstone of U.S. society, and the administration viewed government assistance as an intrusion, as the cause of, rather than the solution to, social problems such as poverty, crime, and healthcare because it pulled responsibility away from citizens and made them lazy. Reagan believed that families were the unit responsible for ensuring that individuals succeeded, stayed safe, and stayed healthy. The administration applauded "intact" families (those that were nuclear and had a breadwinner and a homemaker and so were typically heterosexual, middle class, and white); others received limited supportive government attention. Restrictions on divorce, daycare, and sex education exemplified the dominant politics of the day, as did an emphasis on work of any kind (no matter the

In promoting the idea that government assistance produced lazy, irresponsible citizens, the Reagan administration reconfigured mainstream perspectives on the family and social equity.

pay, conditions, or future opportunity it offered) over government subsidies. Here, in "pro-family" language and policy, were sown the seeds of "family values" rhetoric, which would take root and flourish in the nineties, especially during the 1992 presidential campaign, with conservatives gaining considerable ground in shaping what counted as a "legitimate" family.

The Reagan administration's belief in the free market ignored the ways that variables such as race and class, not to mention job market trends and the effects of unemployment, resulted in profound problems for many people, particularly for the poor and working class, and hardly paved the way for most to prosper, no matter how motivated they were. In his failed 1976 bid for the presidency, Reagan had coined the phrase "welfare queen," which fed on stereotypical images of single black women who were too lazy to work, were promiscuous, and gave birth to "too many" children. These women, however, were savvy enough,

Environmental Justice

Environmental justice movements had their roots in communities, spe-cifically in the efforts of mothers, particularly poor women and women of color, to preserve their communities. In the late 1970s, mothers be-gan protesting corporate practices and government policies that sacri-ficed the health and well-being of their families and neighborhoods. One of the early proponents of such causes was Lois Gibbs of Niagara Falls, New York. In trying to make sense of her son's multiple illnesses, Gibbs began to suspect that her neighborhood was polluted and that the prob-lem reached much farther than her home. Her new antipollution activist efforts gripped the nation in 1978, when she discovered that the school her children attended in Love Canal was built on top of a massive toxic waste dump. Toxic waste was literally gurgling up from basements, and rates of miscarriage and cancer in the community were inordinately high. Gibbs led the citizens of Love Canal to demand that the government investigate the high illness and death rates in their neighborhood and that it fund relocation of the residents. Their efforts resulted in the establish-ment of Superfund, the government policy and funding aimed at identify-ing and cleaning up toxic waste sites, with liability for such cleanup placed on the companies that created the mess. Gibbs became known as "The Mother of Superfund."

In 1982 Dollie Burwell of Warren County, North Carolina, led the mothers and children in her community in protests that challenged both environmental and civil rights leaders, and the federal government, to recognize and address the relationships among race, class, and hazard-ous waste exposure. Trucks carrying toxic chemicals were stopped in their

as the stereotype implied, to cheat the welfare system by submitting multiple claims under different names and by having more children to increase their welfare checks. As this image proliferated and politicians and the media used it to shape public dialogue about welfare and poor families, the public became less and less interested in the truth about welfare (that most recipients, for example, were white and preferred decently waged work over welfare, and that having more children tracks as mothers and children lay on the street before them. Five hundred people, mostly women and children, were arrested at the protest. The event was broadcast on news programs across the country and the environmental justice movement, the civil rights movement, and federal policy were galvanized to address the problems of toxicity in minority and poor communities. Burwell would continue working with grassroots organizations for years after and would organize campaigns resulting in the election of mothers of color to local, state, and federal positions in the early nineties.

In the 1970s, Katsi Cook, of the Akwesasne Mohawk Nation, became concerned about the high levels of pollution that Mohawk women were facing, particularly the high levels of contaminants found in their breast milk. To initiate the Mother's Milk Project (MMP), in 1985 she and her associates trained more than one hundred Mohawk women to be health advocates and researchers. They examined, in cooperation with the Tribes Environment Office, an analysis of how contaminants moved through the food chain—from fish to wildlife to breast milk. Beginning with fish was important for Native women because of its fertility symbolism and its high nutritional value and low cost. After convincing General Motors, one of the known polluters of the St. Lawrence River, to fund the project, MMP found that the river's contaminants were in fact responsible for alarmingly high rates of toxins in the women's breast milk. Empowered with this information, Mohawk families were motivated and informed to demand that corrective action be taken. One of the most important contributions of MMP was that it helped to demonstrate, to Native people and to others, the relationship between the Native community's reproductive health, cultural survival, and the environment.

didn't help women live better). The image of the permanently welfare-dependent mother would last through the next two decades.

In the eighties, an emphasis on the family, narrowly defined, as simultaneously the center of all that is good about the country and the source of all that is wrong with it saw an upsurge similar to that seen at the turn of the previous century. This emphasis coincided with a heralding once again of middle-class values, even though, when adopted by the poor and working class, those values did little to abate their economic problems or social standing. The ability to earn an income that allowed one's family not only to avoid government assistance of any kind, but also to demonstrate or even flaunt such self-sufficiency and acceptance of middle-class norms through consumer behavior, was not only a newly emerging value in American history, but also one that was restricted to a small part of the U.S. population.

The mind-set of the time was often one of victim blaming: Poverty came from a lack of will to work, and complexities of childcare for working and single mothers came from a refusal to be and stay married or to deal with family matters using family resources—a failure of parents, especially mothers. Those families who could not live up to the ideal were treated punitively: Parents were punished or fined for the crimes of their children; drug-addicted pregnant women faced sentencing and loss of their children rather than treatment; parents whose children performed poorly in school were blamed for not being hands-on enough in their children's education. The fact that few families can both be in the workplace earning consumer income and have a mother at home monitoring and tutoring the children went unnoticed by policymakers and law enforcement. The fact that Reagan's zealous military spending absorbed education funding, resulting in weaker educational programs in poor areas, went unnoticed by them too. Materialism and consumption were encouraged in order to foster a "free market economy," creating untold problems for families whose consumer activity was limited. One of the general operating principles of the time seemed to be "there are no problem kids, only problem parents." But policymakers were not the only ones blaming the victims. Those of the middle class were encouraged to see their ability to navigate the economic, education, and healthcare systems as a product of their own efforts and not a result of their privileged social status or access to resources or to the low-wage labor of others that made the goods and services they bought affordable to them; those who could not so easily navigate these systems were seen to be reaping what they had sown.

Treating the very complex issues facing multitudes of real families as merely personal or maternal or moral failures does not take us very far, as historian Stephanie Coontz points out in her book *The Way We Never Were*. It blinds us to the fact that all families are imperfect and that stereotypes and biases encourage us to overlook the imperfections of some people and not of others. And it keeps us from acknowledging that prevention and relief are better for society than blame and punishment. Angela Davis explained in her book *Women, Culture, and Politics* that the strategies of the Reagan administration were designed to deny the existence and effects of institutionalized racism—racist perspectives that go well beyond attitudes of individual people toward other individuals and that are interwoven throughout our various social institutions. From this perspective, she asserted, the suffering of black people in the 1980s was assumed to be because of their own inadequacies, so they had no right to government assistance from programs such as Aid to Families with Dependent Children (AFDC), a program that was severely cut beginning in 1980. Davis pointed out that "cuts" to programs such as AFDC, student financial assistance, health plans and immunizations for the poor, and subsidized housing (which, as noted, was readily offered to white nonpoor families in the 1950s) were not actually *cuts* but rather *transfers*; funds for these programs were in fact transferred to military budgets. Recasting the language of the Moynihan Report from the 1960s, Davis argued that the economic "tangle of pathology" confronting black communities was firmly grounded in the exorbitant U.S. military budget. She showed that in 1986 the Pentagon spent almost $1 billion a day; the same as $41 million an hour, or $700,000 per minute.

In the 1960s and 1970s, feminist, counterculture, and civil rights writers and activists had boldly critiqued dominant ideas of family and community and social relationships. *What else might family and mothering look like?* they asked. *From what other sources might a woman's identity emerge? Could we profoundly reconfigure society?* But this resistance to the status quo seemed to dissipate as the seventies wore on; meanwhile, those who insisted that the current order go unquestioned were organizing in response to the recent cultural upheaval brought

Homeplace as a Site of Resistance

In this excerpt from her 1990 piece "Homeplace: A Site of Resistance," black feminist writer bell hooks (born Gloria Jean Watkins) articulated the ways in which mothers of color have, of necessity, used home life and mothering as a way to model revolutionary power and to cultivate that power in their families. Here, hooks shared her working-class story to push back against attempts to devalue the work that mothers of color do in their homes.

Looking back as an adult woman, I think of the effort it must have taken for [mama] to transcend her own tiredness (and who knows what assaults or wounds to her spirit had to be put aside so that she could give something to her own). Given the contemporary notions of "good parenting" this may seem like a small gesture, yet in many post-slavery black families, it was a gesture parents were often too weary, too beaten down to make. Those of us who were fortunate enough to receive such care understood its value. Politically, our young mother, Rosa Bell, did not allow the white supremacist culture of domination to completely shape and control her psyche and her familial relationships. Working to create a homeplace that affirmed our beings, our blackness, our love for one another was necessary resistance. We learned degrees of critical consciousness from her. Our lives were not without contradictions, so it is not my intent to create a romanticized portrait. Yet any attempts to critically assess the role of black women in liberation struggle must examine the way political concern about the impact of racism shaped black women's thinking, their sense of home, and their modes of parenting. . . . Throughout our history, African-Americans have recognized the subversive value of homeplace, of having access to private space where we do not directly encounter white racist aggression. Whatever the shape and direction of black liberation struggle (civil rights reform or black power movement), domestic space has been a crucial site for organizing, for forming political solidarity. Homeplace has been a site of resistance.

about by social change movements. And by the eighties, the latter were ready to reemerge with a new force.

A "national babble of pronatalism" emerged in the 1980s, as Ann Snitow wrote in her article "Feminism and Motherhood: An American Reading." Political leaders advocated policies and attitudes that were "pro-family," even though they functioned as antifamily for the millions who were not middle class and nuclear. For instance, requirements that those receiving welfare must work, ostensibly aimed at helping poor families become self-sufficient, ensured that poor women would have to accept menial and low-paying jobs if that's all they could get and would have to put their children in whatever substandard childcare they could afford, thus violating the "pro-family" stance that children should be cared for at home rather than by "strangers." Such requirements also ensured that women's low wages would go to childcare rather than to increasing their families' self-sufficiency. Also, a persistent focus on marriage in "pro-family" policy failed to acknowledge the legitimacy of same-sex couples raising children or single mothers who had left abusive relationships or irresponsible partners. Furthermore, antiabortion strategies, ostensibly aimed at protecting babies, and sex education restrictions, ostensibly aimed at promoting abstinence until marriage, would contribute to babies being born into families who knew they could not care for them, and many of whom would then face tightening restrictions on government assistance.

Feminists too began to weave pronatalist strands into their thinking and writing. Feminists' strategies for reconfiguring women's roles seemed to lose force in the social and political context of the eighties, and the moves to radically alter the meanings and forms of the family were, in many ways, stalled. At the same time, feminists were broadening their considerations of motherhood. Though they continued to critique the nuclear family institution, they also made more room for women to speak their own truths about mothering, as Lorde and Lazarre did in the 1970s, truths that highlighted contradiction and ambivalence—warmth and resentment, reward and cost, affection and anger. But the pendulum, which had formerly swung from an exaltation of motherhood to a bold and incisive critique of it, had a hard time settling between these two ends during the pronatalist culture of the eighties. In her book *The Second Stage*, Betty Friedan seemed to retract her 1963 critique of domestic life, suggesting that perhaps the feminist critiques so far had been too critical of family and of the oppressive potential that motherhood held for women. While some feminists agreed, others indicated that feminist critiques of the institution of the family were far from complete.

Pro-family rhetoric and pronatalism were operating within a larger context of cultural backlash against feminism, which Pulitzer Prize–winning journalist and feminist author Susan Faludi identified and sharply critiqued in her book *Backlash: The Undeclared War Against American Women*. Messages that circulated in pop culture, politics, the workplace, and popular psychology served to devalue the important but incomplete list of feminist gains won in the sixties and seventies. These messages argued in different ways, but in harmony, that women weren't really happy with the lives that had been won for them by various activist, and particularly feminist, efforts. What women really wanted, these various messages seemed to be saying, was to marry and have children. They were disappointed with work, didn't really enjoy equality, and were coming to believe that perhaps "traditional" and domestic roles did, after all, hold all the self-determination that they cared to have. The problems that women were experiencing were really a result of *too much* independence, they argued, for which feminism was to blame.

This antifeminist backlash paid no heed to the fact that many women *were* happy with the changes that had taken place. More important, it ignored the fact that the dissatisfaction and frustration that some women did experience were not about their newfound social power; rather, they stemmed from the fact that other aspects of society had not caught up to the changes in women's participation in the workforce. Mothers' workforce participation did little to alter their access to daycare, and among heterosexual couples with children, mothers still were doing most of the home and childcare. Many mothers still were not able to adequately provide for their children because women's wages and opportunities for advancement still were not comparable to men's. Despite the much-applauded affluence of the decade, comparatively little had changed in the lives of working-class and poor mothers or their families. If women were dissatisfied, it was with how resistant social institutions were to adapt to what changes were happening and to make adjustments for the shifts taking place in families.

Friedan's *The Second Stage* was one of the early works of a decade that would prove to be, as Ann Snitow's study reveals, a period of pulling back, of feminist apology for ever having the fortitude to boldly criticize motherhood and nuclear family roles. Critiques of feminism were coming from both inside and outside it, and the pro-(nuclear) family milieu made it difficult for feminists to probe and sift through the meanings of mothering and family and to continue reenvisioning alternatives that were empowering for women. But feminists as a group were hardly cowering. The eighties also was a period during which feminists began to examine more fully the problems of universalizing assumptions about mothering and worked to get more comfortable with the fact that the conditions of women's very different lives created a diversity of meanings for motherhood that were difficult to neatly summarize. This shift meant welcoming conflict and contradictions among maternal thinkers, writers, and activists. The struggle to get more comfortable with difference and conflict was a direction toward which feminism in general was turning its efforts.

Essentializing Motherhood

By the 1980s, "difference feminism" had taken hold. Drawing on some of the biological and spiritual elements of cultural feminism, difference feminism emphasized the ways in which, presumably, all women are different from all men. Among these differences between women and men was women's experience of mothering. Adrienne Rich had argued in the seventies that there was a core to mothering that women could relish and grow from if it could take place outside the constrictions of patriarchy. Echoing Rich and the counterculture of the sixties, which promised unity and community, cultural and difference feminists advanced views of mothering that they claimed held universal truth and solidarity for women. Despite the support for these claims coming from the dominant culture to convince women that they did share a body of common interests, such as being dependent and cocooned in the home, cultural and difference feminisms and their claims of universality began to loosen their hold in the 1980s as women of color, women who chose not to mother, and women from a diversity of family forms began to amplify their voices.

In 1980, philosopher Sara Ruddick published her theory of "maternal thinking," which offered an alternative to the idea of a universal, biologically driven maternal instinct. Ruddick argued that grounding women's mothering knowledge in the body and in innate features of womanhood—reducing mothering behavior and practices to instinct—ignored the day-to-day discipline, learning, and effort that mothering requires. Also, Ruddick posited, a woman's engagement in the "discipline" of mothering—fostering first the preservation of the child, second its growth, and third its acceptance by others—cultivated particular kinds of thinking in women. Women who mother, then, tended to think in distinct ways from people who don't. Black feminist writer bell hooks critiqued two of Ruddick's points. First, she took issue with Ruddick's assertion that since motherhood is not grounded in biology, then men can develop maternal thinking; hooks argued that describing men's nurturing of children as "maternal" reinforced the idea that child rearing and nurturing care were still properly women's realm. Second, hooks critiqued Ruddick's emphasis on parents' focused attention to children, on the grounds that it did not speak to the realities of the working-class day and the depleted energies that parents have at the end of it. Other writers critiqued Ruddick for claiming that there was a motherhood "essence," even though she rooted maternal thought in social practices rather than in biology.

One of the primary arenas in which feminism began to critically assess essentializing notions of motherhood was that of lesbian motherhood. Feminist researcher Ellen Lewin started to explore lesbian mothers' experiences in the midseventies, when few people even knew there was such a category and those who did knew about it only in terms of custody cases and the discrimination that lesbian mothers faced in court. The Mary Jo Risher case, for example, in which Risher lost custody of one of her children when the other child testified against her, was made into a TV movie and was one of the very few stories of lesbian mothers with which most people were familiar. Lesbian mothers were caught, Lewin's research showed, between a cultural dualism that categorized them as *either* lesbians or mothers, but not both. Because mothering was broadly viewed as "natural" to women and because lesbian sexuality was considered "unnatural," these mothers had to prove adequate mothering in custody cases through mothering activity. For lesbian mothers, in contrast to hetero mothers, maternal virtue was not presumed to be inherent but instead comprised a set of behaviors that they had to demonstrate to be awarded custody.

By 1987, things had changed somewhat for lesbian mothers. Firmly entrenched in the family ideologies of the period and having made some gains in issues of custody and cultural acceptance, "lesbian mother" was a category that was recognized and talked about in many circles. Sandra Pollack and Jeanne Vaughn's 1987 collection *Politics of the Heart: A Lesbian Parenting Anthology* addressed the diversity of thought that was emerging among these mothers, with many of the essays continuing from the 1970s radical feminist tradition of embracing the personal as political. Baba Copper's essay, for example, "The Radical Potential in Lesbian Mothering of Daughters," advocated resistance to the ideology of "heteromotherhood" and suggested that the heteromothering rule, grounded in psychoanalytic theory, that daughters and mothers will inevitably struggle in their relationship and that a sign of the daughter's maturity is the distance she keeps from her mother, was a rule well worth breaking in lesbian families. Copper also criticized the prejudice against mothers in the lesbian community, which kept lesbian families from realizing the radical possibilities of mothering. Because lesbian mothering of daughters represented women celebrating and caring for other women, it was a way to resist

"An Open Letter to the Lesbians Who Have Mothered Before Me"

Feminist and community organizer Maura Ryan came out as a lesbian in the midnineties when she was fourteen years old and living in Fort Lauderdale, Florida. In the full version of the letter excerpted here, she wrote about facing discrimination from the general public, which assumed she couldn't be both a mother and a lesbian, and from physicians who assumed she'd be fine with having her uterus removed at the first sign of growths detected there (since, as a lesbian, she wouldn't need her uterus). Mostly though, the letter paid tribute to lesbian mothers whose activist efforts had changed society for her.

When I first started thinking about being a mother, I was watching a documentary where this gay activist said that all gays and lesbians are parents because we all have the responsibility to parent the next generation of queer kids. I fell into a panic, thinking that I was going to be slacking on my responsibilities to help queer kids in the interest of raising (probably) straight kids. I thought that it was impossible to mother children and to mother younger queer people. My biggest fear became that I would gain children and lose a community. I feared that I would be ignoring young queer kids who would need me. I believed that (instead of adding to a diversity of mothers) I would only make myself more acceptable to society while further pathologizing queer women who do not choose to mother. . . . By thinking this way, I had given in to both the cultural idea that someone has to love their biological children more than they can love family members of choice; and the either/or misconception that one is either a mother or an activist—a homebody who fulfills her role, or somebody who cares about social change. I ignored that having our families IS social change; I ignored the social change you created in feminist, anti-racist, and queer activist organizations; I ignored what it has taken you to build your families, and create the change that allows me to have a family. . . . Your choices, your political legacies, and your motherhood battles have made it possible. You are some of the women who have shifted the definition of the word mother, and continue to change the definition of the word woman. You are my sisters and my mothers.

misogynist thinking. In doing so within families that did not see male figures as primary, it also refused loyalty to a sexist and heterosexist culture. Nancy Polikoff's essay, "Lesbians Choosing Children: The Personal Is Political Revisited," addressed lesbian mothers' obligation to resist compulsory motherhood, the cultural insistence that all women become mothers, which erased the possibility for a woman to freely choose whether or not to mother. As a mother herself, Polikoff argued that all choices, including the choice of whether or not to mother, had political implications. Those lesbians who mother, she said, ought not only to dissect the reasons behind that choice but, equally important, to work in very public ways to affirm the choices of lesbians to not mother or to be noncustodial parents of their children.

Separatist lesbian philosopher Jeffner Allen's position some years later on the choice to not mother was more radical. In a spirit more akin to that of the seventies, and echoing the kinds of piercing analyses offered by Shulamith Firestone and Ti-Grace Atkinson, Allen advanced a "philosophy of evacuation." She argued that gaining new views of motherhood would not bring freedom for women; only vacating it altogether and collectively would render its oppression "null and void." Departing sharply from a majority of the writing in the eighties, Allen rejected all claims that motherhood held any possibility whatsoever for liberation and empowerment for women. Only in not having children, she said, could a woman truly claim her life and her world as her own. Allen's view was one among many in lesbian and feminist communities that resisted the essentialism of equating womanhood and motherhood.

Mothers, Employment, and the Division of Labor

Despite the difficulty of challenging the pronatalism of the 1980s and of resisting the rhetoric that feminism had ruined everything that was worth holding on to, feminism and other movements were still creating social change. Between the mid- and late eighties, a number of articles and books appeared that indicated the growing success of feminist attempts to confront dualisms and to begin breaking down gender roles. Among these works were *Time* magazine's "Here Come the DINKS" (an acronym for couples with "double income, no kids"), *Ms.* magazine's "Countdown to Motherhood: When Should You Have a Baby?" "Womb Worship," and "The Ethics of Choice: After My Amniocentesis, Mike and I Faced the Toughest Decision of Our Lives," and *Newsweek*'s "Three's a Crowd," as well as books such as Jean Renvoize's *Going Solo: Single Mothers by Choice*, Joy Schulenburg's *Gay Parenting: A Complete Guide for Gay Men and Lesbians with Children*, and Kyle Pruett's *The Nurturing Father: Journeys Toward the Complete Man*.

Joyce Trebilcot's anthology *Mothering: Essays in Feminist Theory* offered a more academic treatment of the themes that were appearing in popular media. It was one of the first multiauthored collections to pointedly explore the pressing motherhood questions of the time from feminist perspectives. The contributors offered an analysis of patriarchy, and perhaps more important, they addressed how to move from that analysis to envisioning and creating feminist values that would shape family life, rather than values that were driven by men or by the needs of industry or consumer culture. In this effort, they were shaping understandings of mothering that were centered on women themselves rather than on children or on expectations from the dominant culture. The authors focused on developing strategies for bringing about these changes. One of the strategies they focused on was the restructuring of childcare. Precipitated by works in the previous decade, such as radical feminist Pat Mainardi's "The Politics of Housework," published in 1970, and Dorothy Dinnerstein's critique of women's sole responsibility for child rearing in her 1976 book *The Mermaid and the Minotaur*, a concentrated focus on the division of labor in the home emerged during the 1980s. As women continued in employment outside the home, discussions of who was responsible for home care and childcare were increasingly a point of focus for feminists as they argued for a more equitable distribution of household and child rearing labor, especially for women who were partnered with men.

As women entered the workforce in greater numbers in the 1970s and 1980s, many found themselves working two shifts: one at their place of employment and another in the home.

During this decade feminists resisted the idea of a public-private split by looking at how women's increased workplace access was affecting their lives as mothers at home and vice versa. In her 1985 book *Hard Choices: How Women Decide About Work, Career, and Motherhood*, Kathleen Gerson explored the different choices employed mothers were making. As their lives changed in significant and sometimes very complicated ways, working mothers were creating new ways to think about and go about mothering. When choosing male partners, for example, some of them considered how supportive the men were of the women's career and how willing they were to share in household labor. Others learned to reconceptualize widely held assumptions about at-home motherhood and came to believe, for instance, that being at home doesn't necessarily mean that mothers actually spend more time or share more affection with children or that children or mothers are more happy in this arrangement. Still others defied the assumption that as women they should be mothers at all and chose to remain child free. Arlie Hochschild's well-known 1989 book, *The Second Shift*, examined the impact of dual careers on family life, and in particular on husbands and wives, largely from the middle class. She concluded that mothers, and not fathers, continued to be in charge of caring for the home and children on top of their full-time jobs, resulting in a "second shift" of home labor that began when they got home from their employed labor.

Single mothers, of course, were also dealing with a second shift. And they were doing so amid the first presidency in fifty years committed to dismantling existing family welfare programs. The Family Support Act of 1988, for instance, was designed to get people off welfare, permanently, in large part by emphasizing job-skills training and work requirements. While it did offer assistance for job training and funds for transportation and childcare, these were limited to one year and often did not provide sufficient funds to cover costs. These changes to welfare benefits also presumed that the kind of employment a woman could get after one year of job training would provide enough uplift to get her and her family out of poverty, would allow her to independently afford reliable transportation and quality childcare, and would address problems of healthcare and potential care of elderly family members— all of which would be necessary, among other outcomes, for her to be able to survive without future government assistance. The move of many families off welfare and into lives that were adequately self-sustaining was, as a result, only temporary.

Reproductive Rights Activism and Change

A strong antiabortion rights sentiment developed before the *Roe v. Wade* decision was even one decade old. Amid the pronatalist rhetoric, this is not surprising. Operation Rescue, a Christian pro-life organization founded in the mid-1980s, gained notable media attention when it staged mass protests at abortion clinics. Members of Operation Rescue picketed, sang, chanted, and blocked women's entrance into the clinics. But feminists persevered, despite the loss of aid for abortions for poor women after the 1976 passage of the Hyde Amendment, and the nation saw a resurgence of feminist activism in the form of organized movements to defend clinics and the women who used them. Movement activists arranged for women seeking abortions to be escorted by one or several activists, pushing aside protesters who were blocking the entrance and enabling women to obtain the services to which they were legally entitled. Occasionally they even called in federal marshals for protection. Given the violent measures to which some antiabortion zealots would go—bombing clinics, murdering doctors, abducting pregnant women seeking abortions—such activism proved quite dangerous.

The Supreme Court's *Webster v. Reproductive Services* decision in 1989 limited the effectiveness of *Roe v. Wade* by giving states the power to pass restrictive abortion laws. Louisiana and Utah responded by passing legislation that made abortion illegal within state lines, making it difficult for women who lived there to obtain one because of transportation issues or the cost of an overnight stay out of town. On a broader, national scale, antiabortion harassment and violence dissuaded many physicians from pursuing abortion services training, and many who already had the training stopped offering the services at all. Although *Roe v. Wade* remained in place, the reproductive control offered by abortion became a privilege of middle- and upper-class adult women rather than a right for all women.

In response to increasing threats to reproductive autonomy for marginalized women, several groups fought back and formed organizations in the 1980s that would have lasting effect into the nineties and the new millennium. One group, organized in 1983 and named the National Black Women's Health Project (NBWHP) in 1984, was a critical part of galvanizing African American women around health and reproductive rights issues and in bringing their voices and perspectives to the national scene. Grounded in the ideas of physical, mental, and spiritual wellness as emerging from each woman's own informed choices and self-care, its signature "Sister Circle" sessions helped educate and motivate black women about reproductive self-help and health and wellness topics. Within two years of its inception, NBWHP conducted conferences in the West Indies that addressed health concerns of women from the Caribbean Islands, South America and Africa, Barbados, Jamaica, and Belize. By 1989, the group had instituted an international program, called SisteReach, that shared its self-help approach and taught reproductive health organizing strategies to women in Nigeria, Cameroon, and Brazil. Now operating under the name of the Black Women's Health Imperative, and having celebrated its twenty-fifth anniversary in 2008, the organization continues to flourish.

The Latina Roundtable on Health and Reproductive Rights (LRHRR) was founded in the late eighties by women who were mostly Puerto Rican or Dominican. Composed of Latina attorneys, health providers, activists, and educators, LRHRR worked to call attention to reproductive rights issues and violations confronting women of color and to secure their ability to exercise reproductive control in their lives. LRHRR responded in 1992 to Operation Rescue with an unprecedented public protest in the South Bronx—it was the first time that Latinos had taken a public stand in defense of abortion rights. LRHRR later helped to launch the SisterSong Collective, now a nationally recognized and forcible organization of women of color who agitate for reproductive justice. Preserving and expanding women's rights and abilities to determine if and when they become mothers has been and continues to be an important point of focus for feminist work.

"Postfeminism," Family Values, and the New Momism in the Nineties and Beyond

A 1982 *New York Times Magazine* article by Susan Bolotin, titled "Voices of the Post-Feminist Generation," brought the term "postfeminism" into the common lexicon, indicating that feminism had outworn its use. The idea that women were now living in a "post" feminist age suggested that the need for feminism was over, that women now had all the equality they needed, that no social forces impeded their freedom as women, and that any further effort to advocate on women's behalf was just plain unnecessary and may have even made things worse.

Images of supposedly liberated women proliferated in television, film, and other popular culture in the eighties and nineties and the years that have followed. These women were portrayed not only as disinterested in working against oppression or espousing feminist goals, but also as unhappy with what gains had been won for them by their feminist foremothers. Sitcom and TV drama characters were either mockable in their expectation that they should be treated with equal respect and given equal power to men, or they were exhausted and demoralized by the responsibilities of being treated that way. Again, the implication was that feminism was to blame for all that mockery and exhaustion— not the continued inequity, not so many men's continued refusal to take women seriously, and not the ways their lives really hadn't changed much because social policies still did not acknowledge the interweaving of public and private spheres or the great benefit that society sees when families are supported. Yes, women had largely gained increased workplace participation and greater freedom to get out of marriages that weren't working, among other victories. But daycare still was not a political priority, adequate child support and fair custody laws remained elusive, most workplaces still did not accommodate the hard fact that most employees were connected with families that need their managing, and women still earned less than men. If women were exhausted, it was no wonder.

The "postfeminist" idea that the feminist movement was outdated and a bit of a drag was further fueled by popular conservative writers, some of whom claimed a feminist title but critiqued feminism at every turn, such as Rene Denfeld, Camille Paglia, Katie Roiphe, Christina Hoff Sommers, and, in some of her work, Naomi Wolf. Interviews with several of them were featured in such venues as *Playboy, Penthouse, Hustler, Esquire,* and *Details,* as well as the *New York Times* and the *Wall Street Journal.* Women's efforts to carve out an existence that was shaped either by reasonable and attainable mothering goals or by interests outside of mothering altogether were met with a kind of collective eye roll and an unspoken "here we go again" that worked to silence their efforts. But more important, it worked to communicate that feminism was the thorn in the side of American society. The comparative affluence of the eighties was followed in the nineties by a general 4 percent drop in incomes, even as costs of living continued to increase. Certainly the United States had seen economic drops like this, and even worse, but what was different in this time of recession was that corporate earnings remained vibrant. So the drops did not cut across class lines. Some families, in other words, were doing just fine, and they often served as the model against which most others were judged and judged themselves. Meanwhile, corporate leaders in a consumption-oriented society, whose standards of living were not remotely threatened by the recession, continued to churn out bigger, better, and faster standards of living, to which decreasing numbers of families could measure up.

As feminism was supposedly being ushered out, increasing restrictions on women's lives and freedom were being ushered in through a tweaking of the pro-family platform. Far from being outdated, feminism was as essential as ever, as dominant ideologies continued to blame mothers for the ills of society and to create unreasonable child rearing expectations that meant that few women could live up to the "good mother" standard. The 1992 presidential election was characterized by the rhetoric of "family values," strategic language used by both Democrats and Republicans to lend credibility to their very different arguments, many of which had little to do with improving conditions for raising families. That year, Vice President Dan Quayle gave currency to the phrase when he made an absurdly bold effort to blame broad societal problems exclusively on the family and to divert attention away from the role that politics and social structures played in shaping and perpetuating those problems. Quayle's claims set loose a torrent of concerns, news stories, and political turbulence that continue to reverberate about a supposed "crisis" of the family. Quayle managed to link the notoriously destructive Los Angeles "Rodney King" riots that shook the country to the breakdown of the family, and he cited the fictitious television character, Murphy Brown, as a metaphoric example of that breakdown. The Murphy Brown character, in the sitcom show by the same name, decided to have and raise her baby as a single mother. Quayle's criticism of Murphy Brown's willful fertility, much like the "willful sterility" critique flung at white women by Theodore Roosevelt in 1906 and at enslaved black women in the 1800s by plantation owners, demonstrated the continued effort to push women to the margins when it came to determining their reproductive power and agency and to push them to the center when it came to placing blame for social problems.

The attacks on single, poor, and "nontraditional" mothers would continue. In an effort to "end welfare as we know it," President Bill Clinton signed the Personal Responsibility and Work Opportunity Reconciliation Act (PRWORA) in 1996, which ended guarantees of assistance to poor families and required "welfare mothers" and fathers to seek employment or job training and to do so without assistance to help cover childcare costs. Also that year, Clinton signed the Defense of Marriage Act (DOMA), which defined marriage as a legal union between one man and one woman exclusively, undermining lesbian and gay couples who chose to parent and solidifying the narrow parameters of what qualified as a family. In 1998 Southern Baptist leaders held that problems in the family and beyond it were caused by men not ruling those families, and the Southern Baptist Convention officially reaffirmed that women should willingly submit to their husbands. Many men—Baptist or not—responded positively to this reaffirmation, just as many black nationalist men and others had done in response to the 1960s Moynihan Report's similar claims about the need for male leadership in black families.

By the 1990s an emphasis on economic self-sufficiency infused views of women's employment as reasonable and necessary. Most people held, and most "experts" agreed, that mothers' employment did not have harmful effects on children and that daycare or after-school care was an acceptable, even beneficial, environment for children. These positions were backed by research indicating that mothers who worked outside the home spent about the same amount of time per week with their children as those who didn't. They also were backed by research showing that to the extent that institutionalized care of children was injurious to them, the problem was grounded not in the fact that they were *in* such care, but rather in the *quality* of that care. Even so, childcare continued to be underfunded, carework for children in general undervalued, and people providing that care undercompensated. This lack of actual value for the care of children, which continued into the new century, was disguised by popularly espoused positions such as "mothering is the most important job in the world." And it was obscured by the ways in which children came to be considered sacred beings whose fragile psychological makeup and self-esteem must be protected. Despite the fact that most mothers worked outside the home, "expert" advice to parents became increasingly child centered, and families were expected to structure their home lives and economic lives around children's activities and perceived needs rather than the other way around, as had been the case in the past. Even though assumptions that had historically linked children's well-being to women's staying at home seemed to shift, those assumptions were simply directed at mothers in a new way. A "good" mother certainly could work, as long as she manipulated her work life so that children remained her primary focus, and as long as she was willing to take the heat if anything in the child's life went awry. If she moved in and out of the workforce as children's needs dictated, if she was the one whose job enabled her to stay home when children were sick, if she could leave work to attend doctor appointments and school field trips, if she devoted after-work time to both the children's schoolwork and to turning every household task done *by* children into a teachable moment done *with* them, then her access to work or other interests did not have to be impeded. In fact, the more economic and political power mothers seemed to gain, the more sacred the children and the more religious women's duty to them seemed to become. Many women found that requirements for complete immersion in child rearing, on top of workplace interests and demands, were too arduous an undertaking. Up against the sacredness of the child, it was their work that had to go.

At the end of the 20th century, media, corporate, and religious dialogue seemed to adopt the propaganda campaign strategy used before and after World War II to ground women once again in their domestic roles. Nearly eight hundred books were published about motherhood in the last two decades of the century, and author and business tycoon Martha Stewart rose as the media darling, much admired for her ability to create a kingdom out of domesticity. Obsessive media coverage of stories about risks to children, risks that could be countered only by equally obsessive management of every minute detail of children's lives, risks whose countering became the responsibility of mothers, further had domesticating effects on women's thinking, if not their entire lives.

Whether women worked outside the home or not, expectations about mothering became so complicated and goals for child rearing so difficult to attain that women seemed to have only two options. They could funnel so much energy into motherwork that they scarcely had any left to build identity in other arenas. Or they could refuse to be defined exclusively in terms of motherhood and risk being labeled "bad mothers." At a time when "mother" and "woman" were conflated, this meant their very competence or value *as women* was in question. Sharon Hays's 1998 book *Cultural Contradictions of Motherhood* labeled this phenomenon the "ideology of intensive mothering," which held that mothering necessarily should be time and labor intensive, child centered, emotionally draining, expensive, and guided by experts. Many women were, as a result, exhausted, demoralized, and convinced of their failure at being "good" mothers. Susan Maushart explained in her 1999 book *The Mask of Motherhood* that because the image of effective motherhood was so unattainable and yet presented as natural and inevitable, women responded by pretending, by wearing a "mask" of motherhood that allowed them to appear as if their motherwork flowed effortlessly from them and naturally from their own convictions. In their 2004 book *The Mommy Myth,* Susan Douglas and Meredith Michaels identified the links between the institution of motherhood and a media-generated "new momism," which made loose reference to Philip Wylie's "momism" in the 1940s and which they identified

The Motherhood Religion

In researching at-home and at-work mothers, and the mainstream press's treatment of motherhood, journalist Judith Warner concluded that the current culture of motherhood is nothing short of "perfect madness." The excerpt below is from her book *Perfect Madness: Motherhood in the Age of Anxiety*.

> *There's a story we mothers tell ourselves these days, in books and in magazines and in movies and on TV, and even in conversations with our friends.*
>
> *And that story—which is usually told over the head of a toddler, or accompanied by the visual image of a mom making dinner for six while she does homework for four—is that we now live our lives in the totalizing, ultra-child-centered way we do because we have realized that liberated motherhood wasn't all it was cracked up to be.*
>
> *It wasn't good for children and it wasn't good for mothers. And so now we are using all our freedom and choice to set the situation right. We are giving our children what they "really" need. We are giving ourselves what we "really" need—a degree of intense child-bonding that both feminism and Spock denied to previous generations.*
>
> *All of which is good. And right. And, on a very basic level, the way things*

as a descendant of the 1960s "feminine mystique" that was critiqued by Betty Friedan. In the sixties women were presumed to find their complete fulfillment in marriage and domestic life; at the turn of the 21st century women were presumed to find their complete fulfillment in motherhood. The new momism seemingly celebrated and glorified motherhood, but in fact it promoted and ennobled standards of perfect motherhood that were impossible to reach. So it failed to value or support what women were actually doing and needing in motherwork and impeded the possibility that mothering could function as one source of fulfillment or meaningful identity development.

At the turn of the 21st century, the media announced news of

were always meant to be. The only problem is that this story—the Gos-
pel According to Which We Mother—has no actual basis in fact.

There's no proof that children suffered in the past because their
mothers put them in playpens. There's no proof that children suffer to-
day because their mothers work. None of the studies conducted on the
children of working mothers—in the 1950's, 1960's, 1970's, 1980's, and
1990's—have ever shown that a mother's work outside of home per se
has any impact upon child's well-being. (The quality of care a child re-
ceives while the mother's away, on the other hand, has a major impact
on that child's well-being, but that's a whole other story.)

Studies have never shown that total immersion in motherhood makes
mothers happy or does their children any good. On the contrary, studies
have shown that mothers who are able to make a life for themselves
tend to be happy and to make their children happy. The self-fulfillment
they got from a well-rounded life actually makes them more emotionally
available for their children—in part because they're less needy. . . .

All of this research has been around for decades. But somehow,
we've managed to miss it. . . .

We persist in doing things that are contrary to our best interests—
and our children's best interests. And we continue, against all logic, to
subscribe to a way of thinking about motherhood that leaves us guilt-
ridden, anxious, and exhausted. . . .

supposed "mommy wars," portraying at-home moms and at-work moms as in perpetual battle with each other over whose work was more valuable, more morally sound, and more indicative of women's "freedom to choose." As Miriam Peskowitz noted in her 2005 book *The Truth Behind the Mommy Wars* and Judith Warner pointed out in her book *Perfect Madness: Motherhood in the Age of Anxiety* the same year, these "wars" were concocted and fed by news media, and most mothers were not interested in being either militants or casualties in them. Additionally, they argued that the "wars" would never find resolution, no mothers would "win," and most mothers would surface feeling inadequate or like failures, having felt so thoroughly

The Myth of the "Opt-Out" Revolution

To hear the newspapers tell it, mothers are creating a mass exodus from the workforce because they just can't deny the biological pull of motherhood any longer. In fact, that pull is so strong, news sources say and common knowledge supposedly holds, that any career passion, income necessity or promise, or workplace status they may have is no match for it. In a refreshing return to "traditional" values, and motivated by feminist gains that have afforded them the magic bullet of "choice," so the narrative goes, women are happily and freely "opting out" of the workforce and heading home. Given the choice between full and equal participation and opportunity in the workplace and spending their days at home and with children, they choose the latter. Women actually don't care all that much about financial self-sufficiency, retirement plans that protect them in their old age, making use of their degrees, or being really good in their professions—certainly not compared to how much they care about being good moms, anyway. They have come to realize what religious and other conservative leaders have always known, that women find their

Steve Kelley Editorial Cartoon

© Steve Kelley/Creators Syndicate

The turn of the 21st century saw the return of the notion that women find their greatest satisfaction as mothers.

greatest satisfaction as mothers and no matter what opportunities they do or don't have elsewhere, nature is calling them back to the children with a new force. Unlike men, who can both love their children *and* be financially secure, who can invest in their children's futures and their own at the same time, who can comfortably entrust their children to others' care so they can develop other elements of their identities or at least work toward financial stability, women are singularly driven toward parenthood.

This famously popular narrative, which not only populated newspaper headlines but also influenced layers upon layers of dialogue and practice in both personal and professional spheres in the 1990s and 2000s, has become legend. But when we take it apart piece by piece, we find that it is little more than a cultural myth that has some tiny grains of truth upon which we have laid an entire foundation for understanding significant economic changes in women's lives. And on this foundation we have built a larger framework for understanding women's roles, interests, contributions, and needs regarding family and work that will shape family and equity issues in years to come.

It is true that some women are leaving the workforce and that many of them are mothers. It is true that many mothers are finding their responsibilities as mothers to be in conflict with their workplace responsibilities, that they cannot be the kind of mother they are compelled to be and the kind of employee that the workplace demands at the same time. And it is true that when they are financially able (that is, when they are independently wealthy or have a partner who can support the family on a single income), many mothers are leaving the workforce. And if the analysis stops with these tiny grains of truth, the "opt out" story line could almost work But other components of the foundation indicate that to the extent that mothers are leaving the workforce (and they are not leaving in droves, as the media have suggested), the issue of their unemployment warrants a more thorough examination than simply dismissing it as a matter of women's freely exercised "choice." It is important to note first and foremost that mothers are being *pushed* out of the workforce. Research indicates that most of the women who leave do so reluctantly, and often after having tried, unsuccessfully, to arrange work hours, responsibilities, and opportunities that did not acutely penalize them for having family responsibilities. Research also indicates that women with children pay a clear

continued

continued from previous page

"motherhood penalty" that is related to bias against them for the perceived distractions their children present. Mothers also are being pushed out by an inflexible workplace that has not accommodated the changing family. To receive full-time pay, benefits, and opportunities, workers are increasingly expected, especially in white-collar positions, to work more than forty hours per week, and they are unable to flex their hours according to needs of sick children, school days that end in the early afternoon, and summers that require several months of care or supervised activity that is rarely available, even if it is affordable, which for most families it is not. Additionally, significantly increased demands on families in general and mothers in particular to spend more and more time, energy, and money on children have made it nearly impossible to meet expectations for a day's worth of employment and mothering in a single day. Faced with these seemingly insurmountable obstacles, the absence of adequate government support for families' changing needs, a gendered division of labor that continues to saddle women with a majority of home and childcare no matter their work schedules, and media's insistence that if they leave the workforce their "choice" is purely self-directed, many women have left paid employment. And although many of them plan to take it up again when the children get older, they will do so at marked financial and status disadvantages that will negatively affect their earning potential, their investment and retirement plans, and their opportunities for advancement and job security. Plus, the chances of their being able to adequately support their own children, especially given that young adults are dependent on parents later and later into adulthood, are painfully slim. Minimizing the significance of women's moving out of the workforce by suggesting that they have simply "opted out," even if temporarily, ignores these critical issues and diverts attention away from the serious problem of women's unemployment and how public policy could mediate it.

dissected and criticized by the "other" mothers. Some mother advocacy organizations fought back actively by creating a petition to be delivered to major media giants. MomsRising.org and Mothers Ought to Have Equal Rights (MOTHERS) partnered in a project they called a "ceasefire," which criticized the media creation of the so-called wars. They pegged the mythical conflict between the moms as a strategic but effective distraction from the real needs facing real mothers and as a tool that divides women and weakens their efforts to demand change. The cease-fire encouraged women to foster connections rather than "ill will," to refuse to choose sides, and to recognize that few women are exclusively at-home or at-work moms since most who are not in the workforce reenter it at some level later, even if temporarily or part-time. The petition was directed at NBC, CBS, and ABC and culminated around Mother's Day in 2006. In January of the following year, at the Women's Media Center in New York City, MOTHERS hosted a media event in which it announced that its petition was supported by thousands of signers who didn't want any more articles or shows that directed attention away from demands for support for families, mothers, and caregiving. The "mommy wars," the continued political emphasis on "family values" coupled with continued political refusal to support families, and a scathing critique of poor mothers through popular images of "crack mothers" directed women's attentions toward the private sphere and each other and directed everyone's attention away from the public sphere and from agitating for changes in social structure that would actually help mothers and their families. Feminist writing and activism focused, in the decades surrounding the turn of the new century, on illuminating the ways that the public sphere shapes the private sphere and on directing women's critiques at social policy and cultural attitudes rather than at each other.

Motherhood as Contested Terrain as the Century Turns

During the 1990s and the 2000s feminists offered the most concentrated and sustained critiques yet of child rearing standards and their implications for mothers at the same time that they began to explore more fully the broader life of mothering, to speak mother's truths, and to tell, in maternal scholar Andrea O'Reilly's words, the "(m)other side of the story." In the nineties these stories were largely celebrations of mothering. Working-class women and women of color, in particular, made an effort to speak in voices different from those of the white, middle-class women whose 1960s and 1970s critiques of family life did not illuminate their experiences. Books such as the 1991 anthology *Double Stitch: Black Women Write About Mothers and Daughters* and Cecelie Berry's 2004 *Rise Up Singing: Black Women Writers on Motherhood* responded to this desire.

One of the most important texts in the 20th century to address the ideology of mothering from a firm grounding in feminist theory and to apply a perspective of intersectionality is *Mothering: Ideology, Experience, and Agency*, edited by Evelyn Nakano Glenn, Grace Chang, and Linda Rennie Forcey. The book's various chapters, written by noted feminist scholars and historians such as Patricia Hill Collins, Rickie Solinger, Eileen Boris, Barbara Christian, and Barbara Katz Rothman, among others, addressed broad cultural, class, historical, and ethnic variation in mothering and confronted the ways that meanings of mothering are "contested." That is, such meanings give rise to struggle and disagreement over definitions of mothering and the conditions in which it is carried out. Patricia Hill Collins's essay, for example, argued that the right to *not* mother—to preserve access to contraception and abortion—often is not the primary reproductive control issue for women of color. They have historically been more concerned with *having* the children they choose, rather than being forced to produce children through slavery or rape or forced to stop producing children through sterilization; *keeping* their children, rather than seeing them sent off to assimilation boarding schools, sold off as slaves, or taken from them because their nonwhite mothering practices are distrusted; and *raising* their children in ways they've determined are best for their families, rather than having their cultural values, histories, and ways of speaking denigrated in schools, public policy, and other institutions such as healthcare and media.

Continuing examinations of mothering as contested terrain, feminists looked in the 1990s and 2000s at mothering and globalization. Barbara Ehrenreich and Arlie Russell Hochschild's book *Global Woman* pointed to the ways in which mothering in first-world countries such as the United States is intricately tied to economic and social conditions for women in developing nations. Women from such nations are forced to seek work in first-world countries, and they find work most typically as nannies, maids, and sex workers. The availability and affordability of maids and nannies enable women of some means to outsource their carework, which serves, among other functions, to acquit society of its obligations to support children and families, to absolve male partners of their share of the responsibility for that work, and to support the ideology of intensive mothering by making unreasonable standards of home and childcare attainable, even if only for some. Jane Jeong Trenka, Julia Chinyere Oparah, and Sun Yung Shin's 2006 *Outsiders Within: Writing on Transracial Adoption* and Barbara Katz Rothman's *Weaving a Family: Untangling Race and Adoption* examined the contested terrain of mothering for adoptive mothers and the ways in which who "gets to count" as a mother remains a subject of debate and emotional conflict. The important contribution of these works was to direct attention to the ways that American motherhood is interwoven with motherhood globally, especially to the ways that many mothers are driven by economic and political circumstance to leave their own children and families to help more privileged women in the U.S. stay with and care for theirs.

In the new century more feminist writing began to look squarely at the conflicted feelings women had toward motherhood and occasionally even at the (not particularly conflicted) dissatisfaction that they felt. An explosion of writing about the everyday world of mothering worked against a pristine and stilted view of carework as nothing but rewarding and simple and marked by clear goals and notable payoff. Feminist writers saw this as an opportunity to tell the truth about mothering as they saw it, to demonstrate how their identities were rooted in mothering only in part, and to explore how mothering for them was the result of experiences and knowledges they had cobbled together from their own lives rather than from some set of universal truths that all women have in common. This style of writing was marked by a notable admission of the messiness of mothering, the ambivalence women have about it, and the profound challenges of raising children while trying to be defined by more than motherhood. Ariel Gore, a primary foremother of this literary move, wrote, cowrote, and coedited several books on mothering that were part of this genre, one of which, *The Mother Trip: Hip Mama's Guide to Staying Sane in the Chaos of Motherhood,* had its roots in an early zine that grew into an official magazine that grew into a web presence, Hip Mama. *Hip Mama* and the similar *Mothers Who Think,* edited by Camille Peri and Kate Moses, stimulated the literary genre of the "momoir." Multiple print and web writers are now part of this genre, including Ayun Halliday, Bee Lavender, Andrea Buchanan, Faulkner Fox, Ayelet Waldman, Kristin Maschka, and countless "mommy bloggers."

Feminism has come to a place where its treatments of mothering no longer focus mostly on patriarchy and the institution of motherhood. Feminists have broadened the scope of their explorations to consider intersecting identities and oppressions, to openly contest the terrain of motherhood, and to consider the activity and experience of mothering from the point of view of mothers themselves. Feminists have directed this heightened focus on mothers and mothering toward organizing communities that agitate for change. The first decade of the new century has seen an explosion of mother communities, both live and online, that stand on the premise that mothers' lives are worth celebrating, learning from, and improving, not simply because of what that does for children, but because of what it does for women themselves.

CHAPTER 5

MOTHERS MOVING FORWARD

THE YEARS SURROUNDING THE TURN OF THE NEW CENTURY have seen a notable expansion of attention to mothering, motherhood, and mothers. Some of this attention takes the form of continued analyses of motherhood as an institution, as noted in the previous chapter, and some is grounded in concern for children and the ways that economics, consumerism, education, and health and safety affect their lives. But perhaps the most recent and sustained focus of this expanded attention is on mothers themselves. The number of websites and blogs alone that relate to mothers is astounding, and web community and social networking sites continue to proliferate. It is nearly impossible to calculate the number, magnitude, and impact of organizations and websites now targeted to mothers. Online communities, social networking options, and mothers' or children's advocacy groups and activist efforts have grown exponentially since the beginning of the 21st century. And the interrelationship of maternal advocacy, mother activism, and web presence is so strong that it has become nearly impossible for an organization or group to grow, secure needed resources, and flourish without a presence online.

Community and networking sites often overlap with live groups that meet in person or otherwise rally for change, so sometimes it's

This chapter was written with the assistance of Stephanie Langley-Earhart.

difficult to distinguish a mothers' "website" from a "group." Mother sites do typically generate mother communities; sometimes these are virtual and sometimes not, sometimes leading to online activism, sometimes to local and community-based activist struggle. Other times they lead to a focus on personal identity and offer a voice of resistance as they reject the idea that mother knowledge and wit reside anywhere besides among mothers.

Initiating Change for Others: Maternalist Activism

Like the maternalist activists of the 19th century, and like some environmental, peace and family activists (for example, Mothers Against Drunk Driving) of the 20th century, women activists in the current century have invoked maternal authority in an effort to bring about change for their families and their communities. Drawing on their assumed role as caretakers of others, and sometimes on the presumption of their natural ability to ascertain and meet the needs of others, these women, referred to by feminist theorists as "motherist" or "maternalist," use their common experiences as mothers to unite them and provide motivation toward action. Feminist theorist and mother Patrice DiQuinzio explains in her article "The Politics of the Mothers' Movement in the United States" that some of these women may galvanize on the grounds that through their motherwork they learn or adopt a particular set of perspectives and skills that easily translate into carework on a broader scale. Others may contend that as they raise children they confront the problems and inadequacies of current social and political systems and are then motivated to become active to address these problems. And still others may determine, given the strong social expectation that the mothering of children ought rightly to be their primary concern, that if their arguments for change and the betterment of society are framed in maternal terms, they are more likely to receive the attentions and affections of the media, local and national government, and policymakers. Regardless of which, or which combination, of these motivators drives particular mothers to act, maternalist activism is that which advocates on behalf of others.

Though maternalist politics is not necessarily viewed by its proponents as inconsistent with or in opposition to feminist goals, these activists typically view their work as separate from feminism.

Some maternalist activists have channeled their efforts into combating problems of violence in their communities. They focus on raising awareness in their communities about street and/or gang violence and the accountability of law enforcement, government officials, and community members in ending it. United Mothers Opposing Violence Everywhere (UMOVE), a Toronto-based organization comprising mothers who have lost their sons to street violence, was founded in 2001 by Audette Sheppard when her son was shot to death in his neighborhood. UMOVE members promote alternatives to violence such as problem-solving tools and support mothers who have lost their children to street bloodshed. They offer a motivational example of community organizing that engages local politicians through their citywide UMOVE day of nonviolence. These activists assume that mothers speaking out and taking the lead on making their communities safe are central elements in antiviolence efforts. A similar organization, Mothers in Charge, was founded by Dorothy Johnson-Speight in Philadelphia when her son was killed over a parking space dispute in 2001. The organization now has chapters in New York, Atlantic City, and other cities, the energies of which, as its website notes, are fueled by mothers (and grandmothers, sisters, and aunts) who, after the loss of a daughter, son, or loved one to violence, believe that they "can and must be the catalyst for change." The group's mission includes addressing such problems as violence prevention, youth education and intervention, legislative change, and grief support.

Maternalist activism has followed various routes to protecting children and families. The Motherhood Project, for example, is driven by concern for the ways in which living in a consumer-driven culture affects family life and children's development. The group is particularly troubled by the aggressive advertising and marketing that confront children every day. Comprising mothers from diverse races, political affiliations, and backgrounds, the organization works

Mothers' Code for Advertisers

Committed to combating the "bottom line thinking" and "market values" that are saturating U.S. culture, and children's lives in particular, The Motherhood Project (www.motherhoodproject.org) calls pointed attention to the role that advertising plays in shaping the ways that children think and live. The organization developed the following minimum standards and urges advertisers to endorse them as part of their business ethic:

1. No advertising, marketing, or market research in schools, including high schools.

2. No targeting of advertising and marketing at children under the age of eight.

3. No product placement in movies and media programs targeted at children and adolescents.

4. No behavioral science research to develop advertising and marketing aimed at children and adolescents.

5. No advertising and marketing directed at children and adolescents that promote an ethic of selfishness and a focus on instant gratification.

6. Good faith efforts to reduce sponsorship of gratuitously sexual and/or violent programming likely to be watched by children.

to educate mothers about the complexity of raising children in an era that is structured by "the values of commerce and technology" and to encourage them to demand change. Informed by such notable feminist media critics as Dr. Jean Kilbourne, the Motherhood Project developed a "Mothers' Code for Advertisers" and has worked in conjunction with the Campaign for a Commercial-Free Childhood. In 2005, the Motherhood Project collaborated with the Mother's Council of the

Institute for American Values to conduct a survey of 2,000 mothers from all over the country. These mothers came from a wide diversity of racial, ethnic, and economic backgrounds and represented a variety of family structures and employment circumstances. The study revealed that, though the mothers noted several concerns overall, three key issues were particularly significant for them. They wanted more attention to be paid to family violence on one hand and healthy marriages on the other; they wanted mothers' financial security to be more pointedly addressed; and they wanted flexible employment that enabled them to care for their families and nurture other relationships. This survey of mothers' personal and maternal needs and concerns suggests that the Motherhood Project is extending its work beyond maternalist activism alone to focus on mothers themselves.

Other maternalist groups are looking at issues of social justice and the ways that its unequal distribution affects children and families. Mothers on the Move (MOM), or Madres en Movimiento, was birthed in 1992 in the South Bronx by women demanding equity on their children's behalf. Responding to the needs of families in the largely immigrant population there, MOM has directed its efforts for local impact into areas such as immigrant rights, fair housing, economic justice, and education justice. One of its major projects has been urban school reform. MOM members were fed up with the substandard educations offered in New York City schools in low-income neighborhoods and communities of color. And they agitated relentlessly and successfully for change. Their efforts to hold school district leadership accountable have improved the quality of education in their schools, increased achievement scores, ousted corrupt officials, and installed supportive members on the school board. They created a system in which the school district had to act transparently so that parents could see and understand its operations and could more effectively shape the schools that their taxes were funding and their children were attending. Though it has faced several setbacks and troubling conflict, MOM's accomplishments continue; it is a successful model for grassroots organizing and a promising example of how mothers continue to

Mothers on the Move uses motherhood as a platform for working on issues such as immigrant rights, fair housing, environmental justice, and urban school reform.

galvanize on behalf of their families and communities. In a related way, the Children's Defense Fund focuses on improving children's life options and chances for adult success through its Cradle to Prison Pipeline education campaign. The campaign can aid maternal activists and help them galvanize communities by showing how the Pipeline relates to early childhood education and comprehensive health and mental health coverage, how it affects mothers and their children, and what they can do about it.

Other maternalists work to ensure the health, education, and safety of children on a global scale. One U.S.–based organization that focuses on global issues is Mothers Acting Up (MAU), a group that originated in Boulder, Colorado, and now has membership throughout the country. Recognizing that resources are not evenly distributed around the world and that this has a negative impact on the well-being of most children, MAU agitates for policy changes that would eradicate malnutrition, disease, poverty, overuse of natural resources, and child casualties of war. MAU sees mothers as central and powerful agents in this work; the group uses the term "mothers" broadly to refer to "mothers and others, on stilts or off, who exercise protective care over someone smaller." The reference to stilts calls attention to one of the group's signature strategies: Events and workshops typically feature someone in costume and on stilts, which not only grabs attention but also visually challenges the distinctions between mothers, others, and those who are smaller. Using the call BE EXUBERANT! as one of its organizing strategies shapes not only the playful and engaging qualities of the group's events but also articulates its focus on positive change. For example, MAU developed a twist on the idea of a boycott as an alternative way to use economic power to promote change. Its "girlcott" events encourage people to purposely and visibly patronize businesses that use pro-child or family-friendly principles and practices such as offering a living wage, refusing to profit from child labor, or committing to fair trade standards. Another MAU initiative, on which it collaborates with Global Action for Children (GAC), is Stand for the World's Children. This initiative, endorsed by South African Archbishop Desmond Tutu, is directed locally and globally: It focuses on training individuals and communities for grassroots organizing that makes a global impact. The initiative offers organizing tips for rallying communities, connecting with media, and engaging political representatives. The downloadable "Mother Leaders Mamafesto" organizing kit includes community member pledge cards, "recipes" for action, and a personal contact person and advocate within the organization.

Demanding Reproductive Justice

The reproductive justice movement includes attention to contraception, abortion rights, and sterilization abuse, as well as pregnancy and prenatal care and childbirth. What unites women working in these diverse areas is the shared belief that women have a right to self-determination, that they should be able to be intentional about whether or not, when, and how they choose to become mothers, and that they should have access to the resources that enable that determination and intention. Activists involved in this justice work have focused on ensuring that contraceptive methods are legal and safe for all women who seek them; that poor, immigrant, or otherwise marginalized women are not used to "test" the safety of those methods and are not reduced to using the least safe methods simply because they are the most affordable; that pregnancy and prenatal care are reliable, affordable, and effective so that women and children have the best opportunity for a healthy future; that all women can pursue reproductive health with privacy and dignity; that women who freely seek sterilization are given access to it, but no woman is sterilized against her will or better judgment; that abortion is legal, safe, affordable, and accessible for those women who seek it; and that women who seek or have had abortions are not punished or stigmatized for making that decision and are able to have honest conversations about it with other women without being ostracized for it.

Reproductive freedom and control have historically looked very different for women who are white or middle-class and for women of color or poor women. The latter have most often been the least likely to experience the kind of reproductive health and options noted above. Whether, when, and how often to become a mother have been sites of exploitation for poor women and women of color, as earlier chapters have noted. They have had a more intense struggle to determine and shape their own fertility, reproductive health, and family size. And they have seen concentrated efforts by dominant groups to take their children from them either literally (by labeling them unfit mothers) or figuratively (by erasing their heritage in educational settings or restricting the mother's rights to teach and uphold their own cultural values). Further, mainstream feminism's emphasis on the right of access to abortion, and even to sterilization, has ignored the ways both of these methods have been used coercively or forcibly to control the fertility of poor women and women of color against their wishes. In response, women of color have put themselves at the forefront of reproductive justice activism.

The National Latina Institute for Reproductive Health (NLIRH), established in 1994, was informed by grassroots-level concerns from its beginning. Its mission is to ensure that Latinas and their families

receive the quality and range of reproductive healthcare to which they
are entitled as a basic human right. A majority of those immigrating
to the United States are Latino, and nearly half of Latinos living in the
United States are immigrants. There is a close relationship between the
needs of Latino women and those of immigrant women more generally
in that they frequently face low incomes, restricted opportunity, and
linguistic and cultural barriers. These obstacles make reproductive health
knowledge difficult to acquire and reproductive health and well-being
difficult to maintain. Affordable healthcare is beyond the reach of low-
income Latinas; Latinas in general are less likely than any other group
to experience reliable healthcare or to have health insurance. This is due
in part to the fact that the industries in which they are often employed
do not provide insurance coverage. And although Medicaid is available
for low-income women, tough restrictions that vary from state to state
and additional limits imposed on immigrant women complicate many
Latinas' efforts to avail themselves of Medicaid benefits. Recall too that
the Hyde Amendment greatly limits poor women's access to abortion.
In response to these impediments, and in an effort to amplify Latina
voices in shaping society, the NLIRH focuses on national policy change,
education, and state and federal coalition building. It has channeled these
efforts into a "blueprint for action" that addresses issues such as family
planning and contraception access; unbiased health research; sexuality
education; immigration reform; and healthcare services that are culturally
and linguistically competent, affordable, and accessible. The NLIRH
has generated other organizations such as the Colorado Organization
for Latina Opportunity and Reproductive Rights (COLOR), which
provides education and advocacy for Latinas and their families. Run by
and directed at young Latinas, its mission is to "organize a sisterhood
of Latinas" and to promote reproductive education, health, and justice
through civic engagement and community and political leadership.
COLOR advocates for Latinas who are economically disadvantaged
and those who are otherwise underserved or feel they have no voice.
It also supports and advocates on behalf of Latinas of diverse sexual
orientations.

Ideas for Reproductive Justice Activism

1. Get informed about universal healthcare and how it relates to reproductive control. Learn where your community needs help in fighting for reproductive justice. Several organizations offer helpful information and ideas that you can access online. Health Care for All (www.hcfa.org) and Universal Health Care Action Network (www.uhcan.org) are a few of these.

2. Teach yourself about the importance of prenatal care for women and families. One place to start in your search for information is the Centers for Disease Control and Prevention (www.cdc.gov).

3. Research your state's law on breastfeeding in public and advocate for a federally protected right to breastfeed in public places. Create stickers/signs that say MOM FRIENDLY OR BREASTFEEDING FRIENDLY and ask local business owners to display them on their doors.

4. Be a clinic escort. Or be a clinic host: Offer your couch, a meal, and transportation for someone who needs an abortion. You could even organize a network of other women in your community who are willing to be activists in this way. Read about Catherine Megill and the hosting network she created in *Grassroots: A Field Guide for Feminist Activism* by Jennifer Baumgardner and Amy Richards to learn more about this important and needed service.

5. Go to Legal Momentum Family Initiative and browse its Legal Knowledge Center (www.legalmomentum.org/legal-knowledge) to check out or download legislation, publications, and court case information about antichoice violence, reproductive rights, and rights of pregnant women, among other topics.

Another women of color reproductive health collective, SisterSong, identifies as the only national reproductive justice network for women of color in the United States. It is committed to collaborating across ethnicities. Formed in 1997 through a Ford Foundation grant, the collective works to change policy, advocate for women of color, and ensure adequate health education at local, national, and international levels. Like the NLIRH and COLOR, it works on community, state, and national levels, promotes leadership at these levels by women of color, and fights for women's reproductive self-determination. A similarly vibrant and vocal organization, INCITE! Women of Color Against Violence, focuses part of its larger antiviolence efforts on reproductive control, and particularly the violent effects that racist contraception and sterilization abuses have had on communities of color. In addition to the fact that women of color have historically been (and continue to be) especially targeted by coercive attempts to sterilize them, they also have been targeted for contraception that may be unsafe. INCITE! notes that Depo-Provera, the single-injection birth control method, was tested by its manufacturer, Upjohn Company, on women of color in the United States and around the world and without thoroughly informing women of its risks. The shot is now more likely to be recommended by healthcare professionals for women of color and poor and disabled women than for other women. Studies have indicated that Depo-Provera poses potential risks for cervical and breast cancer and osteoporosis, among other health problems. This radical feminist group works from the position that women of color and trans people of color are "living in the dangerous intersections of sexism and racism," and that antiviolence activism must place these problems and their solutions at the forefront. INCITE! develops political protests, organizes rallies, produces a women of color radio show, runs a health clinic, and galvanizes the energy and action of mothers on welfare.

Another area of reproductive justice is pregnancy support and maternity services. Single Pregnancy is an online resource, rich with information about pregnancy, custody litigation and retention strategies, and financial resources. Bold in its statement that it does not "hold the welfare of the baby above that of the mother," Single Pregnancy works to empower single women in unsupported pregnancies and holds the position that all women, regardless of youth, age, partner status, or economic situation, can be good and strong parents to their children. National Advocates for Pregnant Women (NAPW) works on behalf of pregnant and parenting women from vulnerable populations, such as poor women and drug-using women. NAPW offers local and national organizing, litigation support, legal advocacy, and public education. One issue on which NAPW focuses is the way in which addiction is framed as criminal, particularly in the case of pregnant women. Rather than recognize addiction during pregnancy as a public health issue, as many healthcare professionals do, law enforcement and judicial officials have treated it as a punishable crime. Needless to say, this compromises the well-being of both women and children. The issue goes beyond the use of drugs and alcohol. NAPW notes that one woman, for example, decided against an early C-section. She continued to carry the pregnancy and when her baby was born it was not alive; she was charged with murder. Hundreds of other pregnant women have been arrested, and countless more have been subjected to government interventions and charged with child abuse and neglect. NAPW has been a leading force in promoting treatment for addicted women and has kept mothers out of jail and children with their families.

Advocating for Mamas

Few advocacy efforts before the 1970s directed their attentions to mothers and, specifically, to their empowerment. And even then such efforts emerged in tension with the radical questioning of the nuclear family as the core social unit that came from the counterculture movement and radical feminism. Mother-related social justice activism was often connected to workplace rights and equity, racial justice, reproductive rights, and environmental or peace issues as they affected families. But women's responses to and eager engagement with the worldwide web, which has its roots in the nineties but became vibrant and expansive in the new century, have proved a significant force in changing all that. Two other movements taking place at the end of the 20th century additionally shaped mama advocacy and its membership. One was the emergence of specifically "third wave" feminism, which, especially in its early years of the nineties, was focused on individual explorations of difference and identity, an expansion of what "gets to count" as feminism, and personal struggle with race/ethnicity, class, sexuality, ability, and age issues and prejudices. The second was the zine, independent media, and do-it-yourself, or DIY, movement, which directed people to see themselves as sources of expertise and creativity. It encouraged people to break the hold that major corporations and the media had on deciding what was publishable, what was fashionable, what could be turned into a product or service for profit, and who the professionals or experts were. DIY culture pushed people to find alternative ways to create and share ideas, art forms, goods (such as self-made clothing and homegrown food), and services, rather than rely on a consumer culture, big business, and government to tell them what was worth spending their money and energy on.

Out of these early years of the mothers' movement came the popularized use of the term *mama,* a reference that rejects the common uses of the more child-centered *mom* and *mommy,* as well as the more role-centered *mother,* thus embracing a woman-centered, mother-derived, and youth-driven approach for talking and thinking about mothers and mothering. Many of the mama advocacy efforts were designed to represent and create community among mothers in the mamasphere and were not motivated primarily by organizing social action. By some counts, therefore, they don't function as a force for revolutionary change for women and mothers. But by other counts, being able to speak the lives of mothers, using mothers' own voices, and breaking through the elite vanguard of print publishing, thus widening the parameters for what counts as readable and engaging material, perspectives worth hearing, or stories worth telling, are indeed revolutionary acts. It is difficult therefore (though perhaps not impossible) to sift out which uses of the Internet by mother advocacy groups or websites promote social change and which function as a resource for creating community among "the maternally inclined," to use a phrase coined by Literary Mama, and whether these two functions can or need to be distinguished.

Creating Community

Online community building, which had its birth in the late nineties and new century, has provided mothers with a tool for connecting, networking, and learning from each other. Mothers across the country have found themselves drawn to the Internet, and to mother-related sites in particular, for a number of reasons. For at-home moms, live interaction with a variety of other mothers is exceedingly complicated with children in tow. The ability to have intelligent conversations, or at least ones that are characterized by complete thoughts, is facilitated by Internet technologies, though this is limited to mothers who can afford a computer and Internet access at home, rather than those who must use them at public locations, and to mothers who are literate. Equipped moms can log on when it is convenient, can endure inevitable and frequent interruptions, and can nevertheless create coherent online text that other mothers find intelligible and can likewise respond to. Even mothers who are employed outside the home, who may have little or no time between work and home life to experience the company and insights of other mothers, can squeeze in moments with online moms early in the morning, between work tasks, and late at night. The isolation that mothers experience in the current age, discussed by many feminist writers, is mediated somewhat by this ability to connect in cyberspace. Online communities center mother expertise in women's lives and work to affirm maternal agency and experience, and they offer tools for coping with the myriad challenges of mothering in these times. Several offer some blend of webzine, blogging, and feature articles.

Various online groups target a specific readership or membership. Mocha Moms, the Black Moms Club, and Mommy, Too! offer supportive web communities directed at women of color. Members connect to and learn from other mothers in various ways, such as sharing photos, videos, stories, and blog posts about their parenting

Ideas for Creating Community in Ways That Help Women and Mothers

1. Make an effort to build bridges with mothers in your community. Work with the National Association of Mothers' Centers and find out what kind of meeting space is available in your community.

2. Organize a free book swap at your local library, community center, or university. Ask that all the books to be swapped pertain to feminism or mothering.

3. Fundraise for one of the mothering organizations (listed in this chapter or that you know about) by holding a clothes swap. Charge attendees $5 and a bag of clothes in exchange for any and all the clothes they need.

4. Host a mother's gathering or create a mother's discussion group. Delegate responsibilities according to each mother's skill and brainstorm a list of topics to discuss.

and family concerns, triumphs, and aggravations that relate to parenting and families. They also offer a wide array of content that allows users to explore their identities in educational, entertaining, and artistic ways. Much of the content speaks to the challenges confronting black families specifically. Mocha Moms seeks to mediate some of the isolation that at-home moms of color experience by providing a forum for discussion, advice, and marriage and child rearing education. It encourages community service, healthy living and self-care, and facilitates live networking by helping mothers find others who live near them. Mommy, Too! offers articles and essays about pregnancy, family, and work, as well as regular blog posts. Blurring the boundaries between support and activism, Mommy, Too! proudly posts that it is "one of the most sought out resources for mothers of color across the country and around the world." Its articles are syndicated regularly on major news sites such as Reuters and on local news sites across the country.

Lesbian, gay, bisexual, and transgender (LGBT) parents can find support and resources online that speak to their own needs and experiences. Groups such as the Rainbow Babies and the Seattle-based Maybe Baby offer information about LGBT parents' various paths to parenthood, foster care and adoption, reproductive technologies, U.S. and international adoption, domestic partnership law, and parenting for same-sex couples. Other groups blur the boundaries between virtual community building and concrete social action. Mombian, for example, offers political news and commentary, emphasizes legal rights of LGBT parents, and provides information about adoption and reproductive technology; the site's editors also give in-person talks on topics such as online activism. TransParentcy is a site dedicated to transgender parents and their children. Going beyond resources and community affirmation or support, this group works to dispel myths about transgender parents and the impact they have on children. TransParentcy members can participate in educational panels and workshops, and the site is a rich resource for custody issues and other legal matters confronting transgender parents and their families.

Young mamas, who are quite likely to have trouble finding a supportive community and nonjudgmental advice and information, can find community connection and help through sites such as Girl-Mom and the Young Mommies Homesite (YMH). Girl-Mom is a motivating force, encouraging young women who are mothers to "stand up for themselves, to fight for their children, and to empower themselves." Although it recommends against child-free teens becoming mothers, it simultaneously celebrates the capacity for teen mothers to live full and prosperous lives, even as they learn how to be empowered mothers. Similarly, YMH helps to support and inform young mothers in their teens and twenties so that they can pursue mothering confidently. It offers pregnancy information, chat rooms, and blogs. YMH identifies as queer positive, racially and ethnically diverse, and pro-woman; it expressly prohibits posts that are discriminatory.

A single mother may feel isolated or like an outlier in her own town if she is surrounded by partnered or married moms, but she can find countless kindred spirits in online communities created for women like her. Choice Moms is a community of single women who are, or plan to be, single mothers through sperm donation. The group offers blogging, networking events, and podcasts, as well as workshops in New York City, the San Francisco Bay Area, Washington, DC, Chicago, and Los Angeles. Another site, Single Mothers, is for women who "by choice or by chance" are raising their children without partners. As the website of the National Organization of Single Mothers, it offers blogs, message boards, and news articles about parenting, as well as links to other sites such as Single Mommyhood, which offers articles and blogs that address issues such as dating (or not dating even when your kids are). Single Mom offers a community where women can share their parenting advice, inspirational stories, and jokes. Recognizing the economic strain of single parenthood, this site provides information that low-income mothers can find useful, whether single or partnered. They can check out employment resources and education scholarships and find needed resources such as governmental and privately operated food assistance programs, government benefit programs for poor families, drug prescription assistance and healthcare programs, and legal information about child support and custody.

Among the countless mother-related sites are some directed toward women who wish to mother in particular ways. For example, for mothers who strive to live and promote a holistic and/or eco-conscious lifestyle in their families, groups such as Holistic Moms Network, Organic Green Mommy, and EcoMom may be of interest. On these sites mothers find features that vary from video advice from holistic medical experts to a "parent swap" for exchanging children's items, childcare, or green business information to products for sale that are endorsed by the group or offered by "green" and other sponsors. They include discussions of core green parenting concepts, including making (and teaching children to make) environmentally friendly choices, holistic healing, reducing consumption and waste, Fair Trade purchases, organic farming, and toxin-free cleaning and bathing. EcoMom extends its work to local and national activism as it pursues its mission to "inspire momfluentials," encouraging women to assume leadership in promoting sustainable living. While most of the related sites are for blogging or shopping, a few such as those named above are more comprehensive, offering opportunities for community building (including local chapters), education, support, and social change from like-minded moms.

Producing Culture

Other mama advocacy organizations and sites move beyond offering support and education to encourage and provide opportunities for women to be active producers of culture. Many outlets of mother-related culture have focused on literary production and have provided forums for mothers' prose, poetry, memoir, creative nonfiction, interviews, and informed political or social commentary. Mothers Who Think, one of the forerunners of this culture online, hit the web in 1997 as part of the online magazine *Salon,* featuring essays and commentaries by maternal writers on multiple issues regarding mothering, family life, and reproduction. Hip Mama, Mamaphonic, and Literary Mama are three others that have been at the forefront of literary sites, as has mamazine, though it became inactive in February of 2009. HipMama.com, launched as a companion to the print zine *Hip Mama,* offers a more radical voice of resistance that works to represent marginalized voices, particularly those of young and/or single women. Though originally directed at mothers who are single, young, or marginalized, it now has a broader focus but still functions as a zine and community for mothers who do not identify as "mainstream." Those who want something other than "how-to" advice by "experts" and narrow visions of parenthood and childhood find a place on Hip Mama; those who think they're the only "alternative" parents in their own communities find here a nexus of alternative thinking, ideas, and lifestyles. In connecting with other hip mamas, these parents can spend less time defending who they are and more time exploring their identities and embracing the ways in which mothering is a kind of political experience. Literary Mama aims toward no particular demographic but focuses rather on mothers who are interested in developing maternal writing as literature and craft. Literary Mama is devoted exclusively to mothers' voices and especially to writing that falls outside the range of traditional commercial outlets. It features work by talented writers (broadly defined) who wish to sculpt their work beyond blog style. Like Literary Mama, Mamaphonic is geared toward blurring the boundaries that divide creativity and motherhood, and it provides a forum for exploring and sharing mothers' lives as artists. These sites offer a voice of resistance to the ideas that one is either free to create art or is constrained by motherhood, that one must choose between babies or books, and that the grind of child rearing turns mothers' brains to mush. In particular, Mamaphonic writings focus on how motherhood influences the artistic process in positive ways. Its "phonic" or sound emphasis encourages mothers to literally *be heard* by submitting audio files of themselves reading their own pieces or playing/singing their own music.

In 2000 *Brain, Child* was born. Like Hip Mama, it began as a print magazine that has since developed a companion website with articles and connected discussion boards. It offers thoughtful examinations of current parenting issues such as international adoption, the family bed, and frozen embryos. Both intellectually engaging and accessible to wide audiences, the magazine is published based on the belief that mothers are deep-thinking individuals, not just automatons who mindlessly but tenderly execute parenting tasks. It features strong writers varying from prize-winning and best-selling authors to formerly unpublished mother writers. Following in their tradition is *Mom Writers Literary Magazine*, which publishes piercing and authentic rather than sugar-coated pieces about motherhood.

Mothers who participate in these cultural communities, whether as contributors/producers or users or both, not only are released from

Ideas for Producing Culture in Your Community

1. Encourage women you know to submit their own mom essays, photography, music, or other creative endeavors to an online mother community. Mom Writers Literary Magazine (www.mom writerslitmag.com), Mamaphonic (www.mamaphonic.com), and Mommy, Too! (mommytoomag.com) are only a few of the numerous sites that accept submissions; you can search online for more. Think about biological, adoptive, foster, and stepmoms, as well as grandmothers and other mothers.

2. Host a mothers' poetry slam at your local coffee shop.

3. Host a mama art show where you display work by local women artists who also are mothers. Organize an opening night event where activism groups pertaining to feminism and/or motherhood set up booths and artists can meet their potential customers.

4. Use performance as a way to advocate for mothers' rights. Small theater productions or individual art performances have the ability to break through the audience's defenses, especially when related to emotional subjects.

5. Invite grandmothers and great-grandmothers to tell their herstories and submit them to StoryCorps (www.storycorps.org), the national oral history project that gives access to and archives all stories in the Library of Congress.

the tone and format constraints and narrow vision that are imposed by corporate publishing, but they also are affirmed in their effort to weave their art and literature with their mothering experiences and insights. And they are able to do all this in whatever intermittent pockets of time they've got as at-home or at-work moms.

Other mama culture producers have extended beyond literary media to include other forms of cultural expression. MOMbo: A Radio

Resource for Moms was created "offline" in 1990 and was "alive and kicking," to use its phrase, until 2007. On MOMbo moms created podcasts, appeared on talk radio shows, and recorded their mothering experiences for other mothers to listen to. While now no longer active, the MOMbo community's resources are archived at mombo.org. The international network Mamapalooza, part of an exploding advocacy concept, sponsors and cosponsors family-friendly festivals throughout the year that showcase performance, music, and visual arts created by mamas. With a mission to counter the "self-sacrifice and self-depletion"

Photograph by Elizabeth Ziff © Alyson Palmer

Mamapalooza is committed to helping mothers discover their creativity through music and other performing arts. Here musician Alyson Palmer appears with her daughter at a performance by Palmer's band BETTY.

that can accompany motherhood, Mamapalooza is committed to helping women discover their creativity through the performing and fine arts. It creates platforms for mom-branded entertainment and promotes women's engagement in media, merchandising, and advertising to support their own and other mothers' art. Its web presence and its festivals (which now are featured in four countries) encourage a view that motherhood not only doesn't have to impede women's artistic creation, it can inspire it.

Changing the Conditions of Mothering

Finally, just as feminists have sought to improve women's lives, mother advocates have worked to address the conditions of mother's lives. Recognizing the potentially oppressive climate and circumstances in which women raise their children, and how different mothering conditions create different mothering experiences, these advocates focus on achieving concrete changes. For example, working under the assumption that the good health of mothers and family members helps make mothering manageable and avoids economic drain, some activists work for legislative change that ensures affordable healthcare for all. Other activists address such issues as homoprejudice, quality childcare, increasing the value of women's unpaid labor, and changing workplace policies, all of which change the conditions in which mothers care for their families and therefore help to empower women. Some of these efforts focus on particular constituencies, and others work toward societal and/or policy change for all mothers.

Recognizing that mothering is work and should be given priority by communities and workplaces, some organizations and groups concentrate on increasing the value, and the compensation, for the work that women do every day as mothers. Welfare Warriors, a mothers' organizing center established in Milwaukee in 1986, focuses on poor mothers, specifically poor urban women who receive government assistance, and seeks to create change for mothers and their families living in poverty. It teaches mothers how to champion their own and shared causes and provides a "Moms Survival Guide," updated annually, that identifies the rights and laws affecting them as well as "information and articles about the war against the poor." The guide includes names and contact information for politicians, helpful agencies, and programs. One of the primary ways that this group works to change the conditions of mothering is to coach and mentor poor urban women on being engaged citizens who know how to make government bodies work for them. A similar group, Mothers Are Women (MAW), or *Mères ET Femmes*, is a community of mothers who have chosen to be primary caregivers of their children and fight to do so without having to endure poverty and low social status because their work is unpaid. MAW holds that the ability to choose to care for children full-time is as inherent to women's equality struggles as the ability to earn a fair wage. Based in Ottawa, Ontario, this group provides speaker panels, a resource manual that teaches about the politics of unpaid work, and an email discussion group called Virtual Kitchen Table. It focuses on increasing the rights of those who do unpaid domestic labor, and particularly on educating policymakers about its social value so that they consider women's unpaid work when making policy decisions about issues such as economic security and healthcare.

Some groups work to improve the conditions of mothering confronting lesbian, bisexual, or transgender family members. LGBT families find voice, support, and policy change activism through the Family Equality Council, just one of several similar groups. Advocating on behalf of lesbian and transgender mothers and two-mom families, among others, it works to change local, state, and federal laws that restrict adoption, disallow marriage and its economic benefits such as shared health insurance, or fail to effectively address homophobic bullying among children in schools or job discrimination that threatens family economic stability. In addition to seeking legislative change, these groups focus on addressing cultural understandings and misunderstandings about LGBT people and educating members of schools, faith-based communities, and government and healthcare systems. The Family Equality Council also offers a speaker's bureau and a rich pool of downloadable resources covering a wide range of issues, including links that outline specific laws and policies for every state.

The Family Equality Council works to change local, state, and federal laws that discriminate against lesbian, gay, bisexual, and transgender families.

A host of other groups, many of which are interrelated and partner on various initiatives, focus on more general mothering issues. Mothers and More is a group founded in 1987 by mother Joanne Brundage, who was struggling in her transition from full-time employment to being at home with her children full-time; she wanted to connect with other women experiencing a similar struggle. The group she organized evolved through various forms and under different names until it found its current identity as a community both online and in local chapters. Having recently celebrated its twentieth anniversary, Mothers and More boasts more than 170 local chapters coast to coast and focuses on the social and economic value of all mothers' work, whether inside or outside the home, paid or unpaid. Recognizing the societal barriers mothers face not only as women and parents, but also as citizens and workforce participants, Mothers and More galvanizes mothers to act on their own behalf and seeks to "eliminate policies, practices, and attitudes that unfairly impact mothers as caregivers."

The group MomsRising, founded in 2006, grounds its work in the core principles outlined by Joan Blades and Kristen Rowe-Finkbeiner in their book *The Motherhood Manifesto*, published the same year. It focuses on workplace policy changes that facilitate mothers' navigation of work and family life, quality healthcare for children, and attention to children's after-school time through affordable care and better television programming. A similar group is Mothers Ought to Have Equal Rights (MOTHERS), which promotes economic security for mothers and other family caregivers. It focuses on issues such as family-supportive workplace policy, tax credits, social security for at-home mothers, the revaluing of unpaid labor, stronger part-time work packages, and universal preschool programs, to name a few of its initiatives. MOTHERS was founded in 2002 by Ann Crittenden, author of *The Price of Motherhood*, in collaboration with the National Association of Mothers' Centers (NAMC). NAMC offers support by providing online resources as well as arranging for local meeting space for MOTHERS and other mothers' groups in communities across the country.

Mothers Movement Online (MMO), one of the early websites devoted to changing the way we think about mothering with the intent of moving that thinking into social policy, offers a sizable pool of "resources and reporting for mothers and others who think about social change." MMO is similar in some ways to the online communities discussed earlier in this chapter in its offering of essays, feature articles, reviews, links, and resources, but MMO's articles and stories of everyday mothering are pointedly presented by MMO as a step toward concrete change. Many of its articles and commentaries clearly emerge from a commitment to feminist politics. Another explicitly feminist group is the Association for Research on Mothering (ARM), founded by Andrea O'Reilly in 1998. Identifying as "the first international feminist organization" that specifically focuses on issues of mothering, ARM is largely research oriented and seeks to promote scholarship at both university and community levels. It combines academic knowledge with activist, agency, educator, student, and

M.O.T.H.E.R.S. Shape Family Values

MomsRising is a grassroots organizing campaign targeted at changing public policy and advancing an inclusive, family-friendly culture in the United States. Its platform for change is focused on the following core issues.

Maternity and Paternity Leave
Families need paid family leave that extends coverage of the 1993 Family and Medical Leave Act. This allows families time to adjust to changes prompted by pregnancy or the birth or adoption of a child. It ensures job security and uninterrupted income, which protects families' ability to pay their bills.

Open, Flexible Work
Workplace policies and practices should accommodate the fact that a great majority of employees must manage family responsibilities in addition to workplace obligations. A flexible workplace benefits both employers and employees and includes options such as telecommuting, flexible scheduling (such as that needed for children's educational activities), appealing part-time options, and job sharing.

TV and After School
Parents need more after-school options for children, who typically are finished with school before parents are finished with work. Families need a consistent and reliable television rating system they can count on that helps parents monitor children's television exposure after school hours. Given that the hours between the end of the school day and the end of the workday are also the peak hours for juvenile crime, families and communities need after-school programs that ensure safety and foster good decision making among school-age children.

Healthy Kids
The United States should provide quality universal healthcare for all children and, ultimately, for all citizens. A strong healthcare system ensures

everyone's health and well-being, higher job and school performance, and reduced financial burden on families. "Fair share" legislation requires employers to provide healthcare plans. Universal coverage and expansion of government plans such as Medicaid address care for unemployed or uninsured members of society and ensure coverage for all children. Further, attention to toxins in children's toys and flame retardants and to the broader environment promotes healthy families and communities.

Early Care and Education

Childcare costs continue to rise, even as research continues to show that childcare quality remains low. Families, communities, businesses, and the larger society need childcare excellence to be a national priority. A critical number of families still find that childcare that is affordable and of good quality remains beyond their reach. Support for early childhood learning education, extending federal childcare subsidies, and increasing prekindergarten funding can make childcare excellence attainable.

Realistic and Fair Wages

Working mothers earn on average less than men and even less than working women who are not mothers. This "motherhood penalty" is a result not only of workplace bias against mothers, but also of an inflexible workplace and lack of family-friendly employer policy, legislation, and childcare options. Improving living wage and minimum wage laws and prohibiting discrimination against employees with family obligations can address the motherhood penalty and help mothers and others balance work and family life.

Sick Days Paid

Nearly half of full-time U.S. employees have no paid sick leave whatsoever; they go to work sick, forfeit pay when children (or other family members) are sick, or risk losing their jobs for missing work. Policies that allow all workers to earn paid sick days keep children home when they are sick, keep people earning incomes and supporting their families, and keep workplaces healthy.

artist experience and understandings, as well as maternal knowledge that comes from mothers and others engaged in the everyday acts of carework. ARM is the home of the *Journal for the Association for Research on Mothering* and Demeter Press, both of which are devoted exclusively to scholarship about mothering. Another organization developing and disseminating educational, cultural, and artistic information and media about women's lives is the Motherhood Foundation (MFI), a nonprofit organization founded by Joy Rose (also the founder of Mamapalooza). MFI gives voice and pays tribute to the experiences of mothers around the world and honors their contributions to their societies and to the larger world. MFI is committed to documenting the voices of women who are mothers, "honoring and preserving their legacy in perpetuity."

Several new and cutting-edge projects are in their early stages of development at the writing of this book and promise to take the mothers' movement in exciting, multiple, and global directions. The Museum of Motherhood, "honoring the legacy of mothers, past, present, and future," is designed to promote the newly emerging field of motherhood studies and the evolution of families. The museum is to be based in Seneca Falls, New York, and will initially focus on the United States with plans to broaden its scope internationally. The first exhibit, a touring visual display called "Moms Who Rock," was featured in July 2009. The International Mothers Network (IMN), a consortium of national and international motherhood organizations, is the first of its kind in the world. IMN has brought together progressive mother groups aimed at shaping public dialogue and "exploring alternate economic and societal structures." It is committed to a "mother-centered world" and centers its work in and for progressive mother groups who are grounded in feminist perspectives. Having held its first summit in Toronto in 2008, IMN boasts more than ninety-five member organizations around the world.

In an effort to document and publicize the exciting changes evolving in the mothers' movement, ARM and the Motherhood Foundation partnered to create a galvanizing documentary film: *You Say You*

Want a Revolution: Maternal Feminist Perspectives in the 21st Century Motherhood Movement. The film draws from the expert knowledge and research from leaders in motherhood studies and from the expertise of mother activism. It is designed to propel the movement forward, weaving together the contributions of researchers, practitioners, community leaders, grassroots activists, and other mothers and caregivers in realizing an action-driven vision.

Building a Revolution

If a mothers' movement is to successfully empower women, advocates must mindfully consider its goals and approaches. Theorist and feminist writer Patrice DiQuinzio identified six points of concern to which she says the movement must direct its attentions if it is to evolve and succeed. In her article "The Politics of the Mothers' Movement in the United States," she argues that the movement must work to be more inclusive of a variety of women and kinds of carework at the same time that it embraces tension and conflict over these very issues. This blend of inclusiveness and contention infuses the movement with solidarity, but it also avoids a false sense of unity, allowing mothers and others to work together to improve women's lives and to reject the idea that they have to think about mothering in the same way, or adopt identical mothering practices, in order to do so. If it is to be a feminist movement, DiQuinzio says, then the mothers' movement must not fail to advocate on behalf of *women themselves;* it must "require that mothers make demands in their own right, on their own behalf." More specifically, the movement must wrestle through the following concerns.

A mothers' movement, according to DiQuinzio, must first resist the mass media's tendency to use stereotypes of mothers that divide them and pit them against each other. Mothers and mother advocates must examine their differences themselves rather than let the media and policymakers tell them what their differences mean. Then they must work toward a "coalition politics" that builds bridges across differences and find points of agreement on which they can focus in a common struggle. Second, activists must stretch the movement so that every kind of mother can fit comfortably. Mothers who do not fit a sentimentalized image or who are not members of socially dominant groups (such as those who are teen, poor, of color, and nonbiological mothers, as well as those without ready Internet access) must be part of and central to the movement. Third, the movement must refuse to adopt a good mother/bad mother dualism so prevalent in media and in many conservative circles. Mothers and mother advocates should highlight the ways that social conditions and locations influence how women mother and argue for greater supports for mothers rather than allow mother-blame and criticism to direct discussions about mothering that does not meet some narrow ideal. Fourth, movement activists must work to bring young women into the movement. Whether they are mothers, plan to be, or plan not to be, young women need to understand the ways that the institution of motherhood shapes their own and others' views of them as women. Movement members need to help young women know that ideas such as *feminism is outdated* and *women don't really want to work or need work/life balanc*e are myths, so they can help debunk them and open up options for mothers and other women. Fifth, to be a vibrant and promising movement, a mothers' movement must forge alliances with mothers and others who do different kinds of caregiving work. Connecting with others who are involved in the work of giving care to people (nurses, childcare workers, and home health aides, for example) would allow the movement to expand and would more effectively increase the economic and social value of all kinds of carework, including mothering. Finally, the mothers' movement must support reproductive and abortion rights as part of the movement agenda. Being able to determine if, when, and how often to be a mother is a necessary component of women's power and agency. So even though abortion discussions may make a mothers' movement complex, it is critical to make them a part of movement efforts.

Feminism and Motherhood: Where We Are and Where We're Going

The shifting social, political, and economic terrains in the United States since the Industrial Revolution have certainly affected the maternal landscape. Women's maternal experience and identity have changed in many ways. Zooming out to take a broad look reveals, for example, these shifts in terrain: The amplified voices of women and people of color in political decision making have altered social policy. Many women now enjoy economic independence. Discussions about education interfering with reproductive capacity have been replaced by discussions of the right to reproductive control. A wide array of family forms enjoy the support of live and virtual communities. A broadly defined mothers' movement now advocates on behalf of women, and not only on behalf of children and others. To a great extent, it has been feminists who have been at the forefront of bringing about these shifts. They continue to chip away at the institution of motherhood in an effort to release women's experiences of mothering from its constrictions. Releasing mothering experience from the institution of motherhood, as Adrienne Rich noted in the seventies and many feminists have noted since, will allow women to define their own maternal lives, will create a culture that values women's work as mothers and supports them in it, and will give women greater leeway to build identities outside of motherhood. But we do have quite a way to go.

A different view of the terrain of motherhood over the last two hundred years or so indicates that, in other ways, it is still difficult ground for most women to navigate. Zooming in to take a closer look at it reveals that, despite feminist effort and accomplishment, women still are largely thought of first in terms of maternal capacity. Standards for mothering are unrealistic, impossible to reach, and out of synch with contemporary family life. Expectations for what mothering should look like also are often based on middle-class or upper-middle-class life for white people. Men's participation in family life still is often characterized by distance from child- and home care. An image of a heterosexual, two-parent household that is wholly financially independent and has one parent whose time and energy are available for home care and child rearing still shapes what "gets to count" as a family in social and institutional policy. Reproductive control—the right for women to not have children, to support the children they have, to time the births of the children they wish to mother, and to acquire reproductive health knowledge and have access to related healthcare—is still out of reach for many women. Assumptions about separate public and private spheres continue to hold sway, resulting in government resistance to support the family lives of most of its citizens and workplace resistance to adjust to the real lives of its workforce. The institution of motherhood seems to have only nicks in its surface.

The capacity for women to mother in empowered ways is further thwarted by "postfeminist" arguments that feminism is passé, that women are as free as they're ever going to be, and that the status quo is good enough. An empowered motherhood is impeded too by the way that the idea of "choice" often ignores the economic and cultural conditions that women are in when they make decisions for themselves and their families. Feminism has often oversimplified the realities of choice, and those outside of feminism who wish to undermine its goals have used arguments about the choices that women make to justify the status quo. Remember, for example, the idea that mothers are "opting out" of the workforce. News stories about this supposed trend suggest that women freely choose to leave the workforce, and they fail to account for the ways that women are *pushed* out of it, or that most mothers would choose paid employment if they could but are not sufficiently supported at home, at work, or through social policy (such as children's schoolday hours or availability of affordable childcare). Conversations about topics such as opting out, choice, and postfeminism muddy the waters when it comes to thinking clearly about mothering, making it difficult to see what changes are still needed and how to go about effecting them. If women are to live in free and empowered ways, as feminism argues they must be enabled to do, then we must continue building on the foundation laid by women and mother advocates in U.S. history, even as we envision a better future for women. An empowered future for women and mothers is one in which feminist and other women and mother activists acknowledge the ways that the maternal terrain remains unmoved and how women's lives are affected differently by that, so that we don't mistake *some* change for *sufficient* change and so that we can most effectively counter the idea that feminism's work is done. An empowered future is one that offers community to a wide range of families and an endless variety of mothering possibilities. Such a future is open to the perpetual changes that women and their families will face as social, economic, political, and institutional realities fluctuate and transform. It will ensure that the conditions in which women mother allow them to take the best possible care of themselves as they contribute to the best possible care of their families.

READER'S GUIDE

Questions for Discussion

What does motherhood have to do with feminism? How has this book influenced your perspective on feminism? How has it influenced your ideas about the relationship between politics and motherhood?

How does the institution of motherhood shape the lives of women who are not mothers? How does it shape the lives of men?

In what ways are current public perceptions about women's domestic roles similar to those of the 19th century? In what ways are they different? Do you think that the United States has made sufficient progress during the last one hundred years in its views about women?

What do you see as the most significant changes that have unfolded for mothers in the United States?

What do you see as the three most important political issues affecting mothers in the next ten years? Why did you choose these issues in particular? How do you think they should be addressed so that the results best empower women?

How would our cultural views of work need to change in order to best support families? How would increased support for families strengthen the United States?

What is the relationship between feminist maternal advocacy and reproductive rights?

Feminists are not the only ones who have advocated for families. What are some nonfeminist approaches and how have they supported or impeded feminist goals?

How have men's roles changed in U.S. history? How have they remained the same? In what ways have these changes empowered mothers? In what ways have they impeded mothers' empowerment?

How might the contemporary mothers' movement better advocate for, and with, those with limited or no Internet access? In what ways is the central role of the Internet in the mothers' movement helpful to mothers and to the impact of the movement? In what ways is it limited or not helpful?

Topics for Research

Politics

Investigate the current campaigns of three mother advocacy groups discussed in Chapter 5 or three family-related policies now under consideration by legislators in your state. To what extent do women of color and poor or working-class women remain "under the radar" in these campaigns or policies? What changes need to be made so that these women become a primary focus of each campaign or policy? What motherhood issues receive primary focus among these politicians or activists? In what ways does the emphasis on these particular issues function to empower *women?* In what ways does it support an idea of families that is *not* empowering for women or for particular groups of women?

Employment

Compare the family leave, paid sick days, flex time, overtime, "part-time," and telecommuting options and policies of two organizations or businesses with which you or a member of your family are affiliated. How are these options/policies supportive of families? How are they empowering for mothers in particular? What changes need to be made to make them more so?

Childcare

Find two organizations or businesses in your community or region that offer on-site childcare for employees. Explore the history of this employee benefit, including what arguments were made when the idea was proposed and how administrators responded to them. Interview one of the administrators or managers to find out why she or he offers childcare and what advantage it gives the organization. Interview an employee who uses it to find out what advantages she or he sees. What improvements could be made to the program that would help families more?

Producing Culture

Research a couple of artists or groups who are doing maternal art, music, or other cultural production as mothers or on mothers' behalf. What are the artists' or groups' backgrounds? What feminist ideas does their work seem to embody? How has their work been received by the mainstream public or media? In what ways might these artists' or groups' work contribute to the successes of the mothers' movement?

Consider ways that you might be a feminist producer of culture. Create an artistic, musical, literary, or dramatic piece that can function to empower mothers, is expressive of maternal empowerment, or gives voice to experiences of women who choose not to be mothers.

Media

Explore three recent media portrayals of mothers. How do these images play into and support stereotyped views of women and their lives? How do they challenge those views? Some portrayals seem on the surface to offer alternative images of women, but then in the end or under the surface mostly reinforce stereotyped views. Look beneath the surface of the portrayals you're examining and write about the extent to which they do this.

The Mamasphere

Study several mother blogs. What do you see as the common themes explored in them? What themes are *under*explored that you think warrant attention? Research a little more deeply to see if you can find those themes in other blogs. Start a blog that explores the themes that you think need attention.

Activism

Choose a couple of the activist ideas from Chapter 5 and execute them. As you do so, keep track of the steps you took, what worked, what didn't, what happened that you didn't expect, what you would do more of, and what you would do differently next time. Take photos as your project unfolds and keep a journal of your own evolution as a feminist thinker and/or activist. Combine all this documentation to create a "field guide" for similar activism. The field guide can serve to both document the history of your project (an important feminist act) and to mentor future activists (another important feminist act).

Research an organization in your community that is working to empower mothers. When was the group formed? What are its overarching goals and what issues does it address? How is it funded? Talk with the organization's leader(s) to get a sense of its history and its needs. In what ways does the organization make a difference in your community and how could it make an even stronger impact?

FURTHER READING AND RESOURCES

BOOKS AND ARTICLES

Abbey, Sharon M., and Andrea O'Reilly, eds. *Redefining Motherhood: Changing Identities and Patterns.* Toronto: Sumach, 1998.

Allen, Jeffner. *Lesbian Philosophy: Explorations.* Palo Alto, CA: Institute of Lesbian Studies, 1986.

Bassin, Donna, Margaret Honey, and Meryle Mahrer Kaplan. *Representations of Motherhood.* New Haven, CT: Yale University, 1994.

Bell-Scott, Patricia, Beverly Guy-Sheftall, Jacqueline Jones Royster, Janet Sims-Wood, et al., eds. *Double Stitch: Black Women Write About Mothers and Daughters.* Boston: Beacon, 1991.

Berger, Melody, ed. *We Don't Need Another Wave: Dispatches from the Next Generation of Feminists.* Emeryville, CA: Seal, 2006.

Berry, Cecelie S. *Rise Up Singing: Black Women Writers on Motherhood.* New York: Harlem Moon, 2004.

Blades, Joan, and Kristen Rowe-Finkbeiner. *The Motherhood Manifesto: What America's Moms Want—And What to Do About It.* New York: Nation, 2006.

Chase, Susan E., and Mary F. Rogers. *Mothers and Children: Feminist Analyses and Personal Narratives.* New Brunswick, NJ: Rutgers University, 2001.

Cheng, Shu-Ju Ada. "Right to Mothering: Motherhood as a Transborder Concern in the Age of Globalization." *The Journal of the Association for Research on Mothering,* 6, no. 1 (2004): 135–144.

Chesler, Phyllis. *Sacred Bond: The Legacy of Baby M.* New York: Times Books, 1988.

Chodorow, Nancy J. *The Reproduction of Mothering.* Berkeley and Los Angeles: University of California, 1978.

Cohen, Susan, and Mary Fainsod Katzenstein. "The War Over the Family Is Not Over the Family." In *Feminism, Children, and the New Families,* edited by Sanford M. Dornbusch and Myra H. Strober, pp. 25–46. New York: Guilford, 1988.

Collins, Patricia Hill. "Shifting the Center: Race, Class and Feminist Theorizing About Motherhood." In *Mothering: Ideology, Experience, and Agency,* edited by Evelyn Nakano Glenn, Grace Chang, and Linda Rennie Forcey, pp. 45-65. New York: Routledge, 1994.

Coltrane, Scott. *Family Man: Fatherhood, Housework, and Gender Equity.* New York: Oxford University, 1996.

Coontz, Stephanie. *The Way We Never Were: American Families and the Nostalgia Trap.* New York: Basic, 1992.

———. *The Way We Really Are: Coming to Terms with America's Changing Families.* New York: Basic, 1997.

Copper, Baba. "The Radical Potential in Lesbian Mothering of Daughters." In *Politics of the Heart: A Lesbian Parenting Anthology,* edited by Sandra Pollack and Jeanne Vaughn, pp. 233–240. Ann Arbor, MI: Firebrand, 1987.

Corea, Gena. *The Mother Machine: Reproductive Technologies from Artificial Insemination to Artificial Wombs.* New York: Harper and Row, 1985.

Crittenden, Ann. *The Price of Motherhood: Why the Most Important Job in the World Is Still the Least Valued.* New York: Henry Holt, 2002.

Dally, Ann. *Inventing Motherhood: The Consequences of an Ideal.* New York: Schocken, 1982.

Davey, Moyra. *Mother Reader: Essential Writings on Motherhood.* New York: Seven Stories, 2001.

de Marneffe, Daphne. *Maternal Desire: On Children, Love, and the Inner Life.* New York: Little, Brown, 2004.

Dinnerstein, Dorothy. *The Mermaid and the Minotaur: Sexual Arrangements and Human Malaise.* New York: Harper Colophon, 1976.

DiQuinzio, Patrice. *The Impossibility of Motherhood: Feminism, Individualism, and the Problem of Mothering.* New York: Routledge, 1999.

Douglas, Susan J., and Meredith W. Michaels. *The Mommy Myth: The Idealization of Motherhood and How It Has Undermined All Women.* New York: The Free Press, 2004.

Dunlop, Rishma, ed. *White Ink: Poems on Mothers and Motherhood.* Toronto: Demeter, 2007.

Ehrenreich, Barbara, and Arlie Russell Hochschild. *Global Woman: Nannies, Maids, and Sex Workers in the New Economy.* New York: Metropolitan/Owl, 2002.

Ehrenreich, Barbara, and Deirdre English. *For Her Own Good: 150 Years of the Experts' Advice to Women.* New York: Anchor, 1978.

Eisler, Riane. *Tomorrow's Children: A Blueprint for Partnership Education in the 21st Century.* Boulder, CO: Westview, 2000.

Fox, Faulkner. *Dispatches from a Not-So-Perfect Life: Or How I Learned to Love the House, the Man, the Child.* New York: Three Rivers, 2003.

Friday, Nancy. *My Mother/My Self: The Daughter's Search for Identity.* New York: Dell, 1977.

Friedan, Betty. *The Feminine Mystique.* New York: W. W. Norton, 1963.

Friedman, May, and Shana L. Calixte, eds. *Mothering and Blogging: The Radical Act of the MommyBlog.* Toronto: Demeter, 2009.

Gerson, Kathleen. *Hard Choices: How Women Decide About Work, Career, and Motherhood.* Berkeley and London: University of California, 1985.

Gerson, Mary-Joan. "Feminism and the Wish for a Child." *Sex Roles*, 11, nos. 5/6 (1984): 389–399.

Gibbs, Lois Marie. *Love Canal: My Story.* Albany: State University of New York, 1981.

———. *Love Canal: The Story Continues.* Stony Creek, CT: New Society, 1998.

Giddings, Paula. *When and Where I Enter: The Impact of Black Women on Race and Sex in America.* 1984. New York: Perennial, 2001.

Gilligan, Carol. *In a Different Voice: Psychological Theory and Women's Development.* Cambridge, MA: Harvard University, 1982.

Gilman, Charlotte Perkins. *The Man-Made World or Our Androcentric Culture.* New York: Charlton, 1911.

———. *Women and Economics: A Study of the Economic Relation Between Men and Women as a Factor in Social Evolution,* edited by Carl Degler. New York: Harper and Row, (1898) 1966.

Ginsburg, Faye D., and Rayna Rapp, eds. *Conceiving the New World Order: The Global Politics of Reproduction.* Berkeley: University of California, 1995.

Glenn, Evelyn Nakano, Grace Chang, and Linda Rennie Forcey, eds. *Mothering: Ideology, Experience, and Agency.* New York: Routledge; Orenstein, 1994; 2000.

Gordon, Linda. *Woman's Body, Woman's Right: Birth Control in America.* New York: Grossman, 1976.

Gordon, Tuula. *Feminist Mothers.* New York: New York University, 1990.

Gore, Ariel. *The Hip Mama Survival Guide.* New York: Hyperion, 1998.

———. *The Mother Trip: Hip Mama's Guide to Staying Sane in the Chaos of Motherhood.* Seattle: Seal, 2000.

———. *Whatever, Mom: Hip Mama's Guide to Raising a Teenager.* Emeryville, CA: Seal, 2004.

Gore, Ariel, and Bee Lavender, eds. *Breeder: Real-Life Stories from the New Generation of Mothers.* Seattle: Seal, 2001.

Greer, Germaine. *Sex and Destiny: The Politics of Human Fertility.* New York: Harper and Row, 1986.

Hanigsberg, Julia E., and Sara Ruddick, eds. *Mother Troubles: Rethinking Contemporary Maternal Dilemmas.* Boston: Beacon, 1999.

Hansen, Elaine Tuttle. *Mother Without Child: Contemporary Fiction and the Crisis of Motherhood.* Berkeley: University of California, 1997.

Hays, Sharon. *The Cultural Contradictions of Motherhood.* New Haven, CT: Yale University, 1996.

Hequembourg, Amy. *Lesbian Motherhood.* Binghamton, NY: Haworth Park, 2007.

Hirsch, Marianne. *The Mother/Daughter Plot: Narrative, Psychoanalysis, Feminism.* Bloomington: Indiana University, 1989.

Hirshman, Linda R. *Get to Work . . . and Get a Life Before It's Too Late.* New York: Penguin, 2006.

Hochschild, Arlie, and Anne Machung. *The Second Shift.* New York: Penguin, 1989, 2003.

hooks, bell. *Feminist Theory: From Margin to Center*. Cambridge, MA: South End, 1984, 2000.

———. *Yearning: Race, Gender, and Cultural Politics*. Cambridge, MA: South End, 1990.

Johnson, Miriam M. *Strong Mothers, Weak Wives: The Search for Gender Equality*. Berkeley: University of California, 1989.

Johnston, Jill. *Lesbian Nation: The Feminist Solution*. New York: Simon and Schuster, 1973.

Juffer, Jane. *The Single Mother: The Emergence of the Domestic Intellectual*. New York: New York University, 2006.

Kinser, Amber E., ed. *Mothering in the Third Wave*. Toronto: Demeter, 2008.

Koven, Seth, and Sonya Michel, eds. *Mothers of a New World: Maternalist Politics and the Origins of Welfare States*. New York: Routledge, 1993.

Kristeva, Julia. "Stabat Mater." In *Tales of Love: European Perspectives,* translated by Leon S. Roudiez, pp. 234–263. New York: Columbia University, 1987.

Ladd-Taylor, Molly. "Mother-Worship/Mother-Blame: Politics and Welfare in an Uncertain Age." *The Journal of the Association for Research on Mothering*, 6, no.1 (2004): 7–15.

Lavell-Harvard, D. Memee, and Jeannette Corbiere Lavell, eds. *"Until Our Hearts Are on the Ground": Aboriginal Mothering, Oppression, Resistance and Rebirth*. Toronto: Demeter, 2006.

Lazarre, Jane. *The Mother Knot*. New York: McGraw-Hill, 1976.

LeBlanc, Wendy. *Naked Motherhood: Shattering Illusions and Sharing Truths*. Milsons Point, New South Wales: Random House Australia, 1999.

Lorde, Audre. "Man Child: A Black Lesbian Feminist's Response." In *Sister Outsider: Essays and Speeches*, pp. 72–80. Berkeley, CA: The Crossing, 1984.

Luker, Kristen. *Abortion and the Politics of Motherhood*. Berkeley: University of California, 1984.

Mann, Barbara Alice. *Iroquoian Women: The Gantowisas*. New York: Peter Lang, 2000.

Martin, Emily. *The Woman in the Body: A Cultural Analysis of Reproduction*. Boston: Beacon, 1987.

Maushart, Susan. *The Mask of Motherhood: How Becoming a Mother Changes Everything and Why We Pretend It Doesn't*. New York: Penguin, 1999.

Mintz, Steven, and Susan Kellogg. *Domestic Revolutions: A Social History of American Family Life*. New York: The Free Press, 1988.

"Motherhood and Sexuality." Special Issue. *Hypatia*, 1, no. 2 (1986).

"Mothering and Feminism." Special Issue. *Journal of the Association for Research on Mothering*, 8, 1/2 (Winter/Summer 2006).

Nathanson, Jessica, and Laura Camille Tuley, eds. *Mother Knows Best: Talking Back to The "Experts."* Toronto: Demeter, 2008.

Nicholson, Linda. "The Myth of the Traditional Family." In *Feminism and Families*, edited by Hilde Lindemann Nelson, pp. 27–42. New York: Routledge, 1997.

Noonan, Emily J. "The Globalization of Love: Transnational Adoption and Engagement with the Globalized World." *The Journal of the Association for Research on Mothering*, 6, no. 1 (2004): 145–156.

O'Brien, Mary. *The Politics of Reproduction*. New York: Harper Collins, 1974.

O'Keefe, Claudia, ed. *Mother: Famous Writers Celebrate Motherhood with a Treasury of Short Stories, Essays, and Poems*. New York: Pocket, 1996.

O'Reilly, Andrea, ed. *Feminist Mothering*. New York: New York State University, 2008.

———. *Maternal Theory: Essential Readings*. Toronto: Demeter, 2007.

O'Reilly, Andrea, and Sharon Abbey, eds. *Mothers and Daughters: Connection, Empowerment and Transformation*. Lanham: Rowman and Littlefield, 2000.

O'Reilly, Andrea, and Geoffrey Golson, ed. *Encyclopedia of Motherhood*. London: Sage (forthcoming).

Orenstein, Peggy. *Flux: Women on Sex, Work, Kids, Love, and Life in a Half-Changed World*. New York: Anchor, 2000.

Oyewumi, Oyeronke, ed. *African Women and Feminism: Reflecting on the Politics of Sisterhood*. Trenton, NJ: Africa World, 2003.

Parsons, Elsie Clews. "Feminism and the Family." *International Journal of Ethics*, 28, (1917): 52–58.

Peskowitz, Miriam. *The Truth Behind the Mommy Wars: Who Decides What Makes a Good Mother?* Emeryville, CA: Seal, 2005.

Pollack, Sandra, and Jeanne Vaughn, eds. *Politics of the Heart: A Lesbian Parenting Anthology*. Ann Arbor, MI: Firebrand, 1987.

Rich, Adrienne. *Of Woman Born: Motherhood as Experience and Institution*. New York: W. W. Norton, 1986.

Roberts, Dorothy. "Introduction." In *Killing the Black Body: Race, Reproduction, and the Meaning of Liberty*, pp. 3–21. New York: Vintage, 1998.

Rossiter, Amy. *From Private to Public: A Feminist Exploration of Early Mothering*. Ontario: The Women's Press, 1988.

Rothman, Barbara Katz. *In Labor: Women and Power in the Birthplace*. New York: W. W. Norton, 1982.

———. *Weaving a Family: Untangling Race and Adoption*. Boston: Beacon, 2005.

Rubin, Lillian. *Worlds of Pain: Life in the Working-Class Family*. New York: Basic, 1976.

Ruddick, Sara. *Maternal Thinking: Toward a Politics of Peace*. Boston: Beacon, 1989.

———. "Preservative Love and Military Destruction: Some Reflections on Mothering and Peace." In *Mothering: Essays in Feminist Theory*, edited by Joyce Trebilcot, pp. 231–262. Savage, MD: Rowman and Littlefield, 1983.

Silliman, Jael, Marlene Fried, Loretta Ross, and Elena R. Gutiérrez. *Undivided Rights: Women of Color Organize for Reproductive Justice*. Cambridge, MA: South End, 2004.

Silverstein, Olga, and Beth Rashbaum. *The Courage to Raise Good Men*. New York: Viking, 1994.

Simons, Margaret A. "Motherhood, Feminism and Identity." *Women's Studies International Forum*, 7, no. 5 (1984): 349–359.

Snitow, Ann. "Feminism and Motherhood: An American Reading." *Feminist Review*, 40, no.1 (1992): 32–51.

Solinger, Rickie. *Pregnancy and Power: A Short History of Reproductive Politics in America*. New York: New York University, 2005.

Sullivan, Maureen. *The Family of Woman: Lesbian Mothers, Their Children, and the Undoing of Gender*. Berkeley: University of California, 2004.

Thomas, Carol. "The Baby and the Bath Water: Disabled Women and Motherhood in Social Context." *Sociology of Health and Illness,* 19, no. 5 (1997): 622–643.

Thorne, Barrie, and Marilyn Yalom, eds. *Rethinking the Family: Some Feminist Questions*. Boston: Northeastern University, 1992.

Thurer, Shari L. *The Myths of Motherhood: How Culture Reinvents the Good Mother*. Boston: Houghton Mifflin, 1994.

Trenka, Jane Jeong, Julia Chinyere Oparah, and Sun Yung Shin, eds. *Outsiders Within: Writing on Transracial Adoption*. Cambridge, MA: South End, 2006.

Umansky, Lauri. *Motherhood Reconceived: Feminism and the Legacies of the Sixties*. New York: New York University, 1996.

Wagner, Catherine, and Rebecca Wolff, eds. *Not for Mothers Only: Contemporary Poems on Child-Getting and Child-Rearing*. New York: Fence, 2007.

Wagner, Sally Roesch. *Sisters in Spirit: Haudenosaunee (Iroquois) Influence on Early American Feminists*. Summertown, TN: Native Voices, 2001.

Walker, Alice. *In Search of Our Mothers' Gardens*. San Diego: Harcourt Brace Jovanovich, 1974.

Walkerdine, Valerie, and Helen Lucey. *Democracy in the Kitchen: Regulating Mothers and Socialising Daughters*. London: Virago, 1989.

Wall, Steve. *Wisdom's Daughters: Conversations with Women Elders of Native America*. New York: HarperCollins, 1993.

Warner, Judith. *Perfect Madness: Motherhood in the Age of Anxiety*. New York: Riverhead, 2005.

White, Deborah Gray. *Too Heavy a Load: Black Women in Defense of Themselves, 1894–1994*. New York: W. W. Norton, 1994.

Williams, Joan C., Jessica Manvell, and Stephanie Bronstein. "Opt Out or Pushed Out? How the Press Covers Work/Family Conflict: The Untold Story of Why Women Leave the Workforce." The Center for WorkLife Law, University of California Hastings College of the Law, 2006. www.uchastings.edu/site_files/WLL/OptOutPushedOut.pdf (accessed March 14, 2009)

Zimmerman, Mary K., Jacquelyn S. Litt, and Christine E. Bose. *Global Dimensions of Gender and Carework*. Palo Alto, CA: Stanford University, 2006.

WEBSITES

Association for Research on Mothering: www.yorku.ca/arm
Black Moms Club: blackmomsclub.ning.com
Brain, Child: www.brainchildmag.com
Choice Moms: www.choicemoms.org
Colorado Organization for Latina Opportunity and Reproductive Rights: www.colorlatina.org

Family Equality Council: www.familyequality.org
Girl-Mom: www.girlmom.com
Hip Mama: www.hipmama.com
Holistic Moms Network: www.holisticmoms.org
Incite!: www.incite-national.org
International Breast Milk Project: www.breastmilkproject.org
International Mothers Network: www.internationalmothersnetwork.org/home.html
La Leche League: www.llli.org
Literary Mama: www.literarymama.com
Mamapalooza: www.mamapalooza.com/home.html
Mamaphonic: www.mamaphonic.com
Mamazine: www.mamazine.com
Maybe Baby: www.maybebabyseattle.org/Maybe_Baby_Seattle/Home.html
Mocha Moms: www.mochamoms.org
Mombian: www.mombian.com
MOMbo: www.mombo.org
Mommy Too!: mommytoomag.com
Moms Making Our Milk Safe: www.safemilk.org
MomsRising: www.momsrising.org
Mom Writers Literary Magazine: www.momwriterslitmag.com
Mothers Acting Up: www.mothersactingup.org
Mothers and More: www.mothersandmore.org
Mothers Are Women: www.mothersarewomen.com
Mothers in Charge: www.mothersincharge.org
Mothers Movement Online: www.mothersmovement.org
Mothers on the Move/Madres en Movimiento: www.mothersonthemove.org
Mothers Ought to Have Equal Rights: www.mothersoughttohaveequalrights.org
Mothers Who Think: dir.salon.com/topics/mwt
Museum of Motherhood: www.museumofmotherhood.org/Info.html
National Advocates for Pregnant Women: www.advocatesforpregnantwomen.org
National Association of Mothers' Centers: www.motherscenter.org
National Latina Institute for Reproductive Health: www.latinainstitute.org
Single Pregnancy: www.singlepregnancy.com
SisterSong: www.sistersong.net
The Motherhood Foundation: www.museumofmotherhood.org/Info.html
The Motherhood Project: www.motherhoodproject.org
The Rainbow Babies: www.therainbowbabies.com

SOURCES

Chapter 1

ACLU of Arkansas. "Frequently Asked Questions About Arkansas Act 1 (2008)." www .acluarkansas.org/content/index.php?option=com_content&task=view&id=95&Ite mid=1 (accessed November 30, 2009)

Anderson, Kim. "Giving Life to the People: An Indigenous Ideology of Motherhood." In *Maternal Theory: Essential Readings*, edited by Andrea O'Reilly, pp. 761–781. Toronto: Demeter, 2007.

Atkinson, Ti-Grace. *Amazon Odyssey: The First Collection of Writings by the Political Pioneer of the Women's Movement*. Barcelona: Links, 1974.

Bernard, Jessie. *The Future of Motherhood*. New York: Penguin, 1974.

Collins, Gail. *America's Women: 400 Years of Dolls, Drudges, Helpmates, and Heroines*. New York: HarperCollins, 2003.

Collins, Patricia Hill. *Black Feminist Thought: Knowledge, Consciousness, and the Politics of Empowerment*. New York: Routledge, Chapman and Hall, 1991.

Combahee River Collective. "A Black Feminist Statement." In *Feminist Theory Reader: Local and Global Perspectives*, edited by Carole R. McCann and Seung-Kyung Kim, pp. 164–171. New York: Routledge, 2003.

Coontz, Stephanie. *The Way We Never Were: American Families and the Nostalgia Trap*. New York: Basic, 1992.

de Beauvoir, Simone. *The Second Sex*. New York: Alfred A. Knopf, 1952.

Ehrenreich, Barbara, and Deirdre English. *For Her Own Good: 150 Years of the Experts' Advice to Women*. New York: Anchor, 1978.

Eisler, Riane. *Sacred Pleasure: Sex, Myth, and the Politics of the Body—New Paths to Power and Love*. San Francisco: HarperSanFrancisco, 1998.

Firestone, Shulamith. *The Dialectic of Sex: The Case for Feminist Revolution*. New York: William Morrow, 1970.

Foss, Karen A., and Sonja K. Foss. *Women Speak: The Eloquence of Women's Lives*. Prospect Heights, IL: Waveland, 1991.

Freedman, Estelle B. *No Turning Back: The History of Feminism and the Future of Women*. London: Profile, 2002.

Friedan, Betty. *The Feminine Mystique*. New York: Dell, 1963.

Friedman, May, and Shana L. Calixte, eds. *Mothering and Blogging: The Radical Act of the MommyBlog*. Toronto: Demeter, 2009.

Giddings, Paula. *When and Where I Enter: The Impact of Black Women on Race and Sex in America*. 1984. New York: Perennial, 2001.

Gilman, Charlotte Perkins. *Women and Economics: A Study of the Economic Relation Between Men and Women as a Factor in Social Evolution,* edited by Carl Degler. New York: Harper and Row, (1898) 1966.

Grimké, Sarah Moore. *Letters on the Equality of the Sexes, and the Condition of Woman: Addressed to Mary S. Parker, President of the Boston Female Anti-Slavery Society.* Boston: I. Knapp, 1838.

Hays, Sharon. *The Cultural Contradictions of Motherhood.* New Haven, CT: Yale University, 1996.

Hochschild, Arlie, and Anne Machung. *The Second Shift.* New York: Penguin, 1989, 2003.

International Mothers Network. www.internationalmothersnetwork.org (accessed October 26, 2009)

Johnston, Jill. *Lesbian Nation: The Feminist Solution*. New York: Simon and Schuster, 1973.

"Julia Ward Howe: The Woman Behind Mother's Day." *Democracy Now! The War and Peace Report.* www.democracynow.org/2005/5/6/julia_ward_howe_the_woman_behind (accessed August 15, 2009)

Lorde, Audre. "Man Child: A Black Lesbian Feminist's Response." In *Sister Outsider: Essays and Speeches*, pp. 72–80. Berkeley, CA: The Crossing, 1984.

Mann, Barbara Alice. *Iroquoian Women: The Gantowisas.* New York: Peter Lang, 2000.

Miedzian, Myriam, and Alisa Malinovich. *Generations: A Century of Women Speak About Their Lives.* NY: The Atlantic Monthly, 1997.

Mink, Gwendolyn. *The Wages of Motherhood: Inequality in the Welfare State, 1917–1942.* Ithaca, NY: Cornell University, 1995.

Moraga, Cherríe, and Gloria Anzaldúa. *This Bridge Called My Back: Writings by Radical Women of Color.* Watertown, MA: Persephone, 1981.

The Mother's Movement Online. www.mothersmovement.org (accessed October 27, 2009)

O'Reilly, Andrea. *Rocking the Cradle: Thoughts on Feminism, Motherhood and the Possibility of Empowered Mothering.* Toronto: Demeter, 2006.

Pollack, Sandra, and Jeanne Vaughn, eds. *Politics of the Heart: A Lesbian Parenting Anthology.* Ann Arbor, MI: Firebrand, 1987.

Rich, Adrienne. *Of Woman Born: Motherhood as Experience and Institution.* New York: W. W. Norton, 1976.

Ruddick, Sara. "Maternal Thinking." In *Mothering: Essays in Feminist Theory*, edited by Joyce Trebilcot, pp. 213–230. Savage, MD: Rowman and Littlefield, 1983.

Smith, Dinitia. "The Love That Dare Not Squeak Its Name: Homosexuality Among Animals Is Common." *New York Times*, B7, February 7, 2004.

Solinger, Rickie. *Pregnancy and Power: A Short History of Reproductive Politics in America.* New York: New York University, 2005.

Stanton, Elizabeth Cady. "Declaration of Sentiments and Resolutions at the First Women's Rights Convention in Seneca Falls." In *A History of Woman Suffrage, Vol. 1,* 1889, pp. 70–71. New York: Arno, 1969.

Thurer, Shari L. *The Myths of Motherhood: How Culture Reinvents the Good Mother.* Boston: Houghton Mifflin, 1994.

Tucker, Judith Stadtman. The Mother's Movement Online. www.mothersmovement.org (accessed October 27, 2009)

Umansky, Lauri. *Motherhood Reconceived: Feminism and the Legacies of the Sixties.* New York: New York University, 1996.

Wagner, Sally Roesch. *Sisters in Spirit: Haudenosaunee (Iroquois) Influence on Early American Feminists.* Summertown, TN: Native Voices, 2001.

Walker, Alice. *In Search of Our Mothers' Gardens.* San Diego: Harcourt Brace Jovanovich, 1974.

Wall, Steve. *Wisdom's Daughters: Conversations with Women Elders of Native America.* New York: HarperCollins, 1993.

West Virginia Division of Culture and History. Archives and History. "Anna Marie Reeves Jarvis." www.wvculture.org/hiSTory/jarvis.html (accessed July 20, 2009)

Willard, Frances Elizabeth. "Home Protection Manual." New York: n.p., 1879.

Wollstonecraft, Mary. *A Vindication of the Rights of Woman.* 1792. New York: Alfred A. Knopf, 1992.

Woolf, Virginia. *A Room of One's Own.* Orlando, FL: Harcourt, Brace and World, 1929.

Chapter 2

Addams, Jane. "Why Women Should Vote." *Ladies' Home Journal* (January 1910). Reprinted in *Jane Addams: A Centennial Reader,* edited by Emily Cooper Johnson, pp. 104–107. New York: Macmillan, 1960.

Berg, Allison. *Mothering the Race: Women's Narratives of Reproduction, 1890–1930.* Urbana: University of Illinois, 2002.

"Birth Control Pioneer." The Emma Goldman Papers, Online Exhibition. Berkeley DigitalLibrarySunSITE.http://sunsite.berkeley.edu/goldman/Exhibition/birthcontrol .html (accessed November 27, 2009)

Catt, Carrie Chapman. "Evolution and Woman's Suffrage." Manuscript of a speech delivered May 18, 1893, in Catt Collection, New York Public Library.

Chase, Susan E., and Mary F. Rogers. *Mothers and Children: Feminist Analyses and Personal Narratives.* New Brunswick, NJ: Rutgers University, 2001.

Chen, Constance M. *"The Sex Side of Life": Mary Ware Dennett's Pioneering Battle for Birth Control and Sex Education.* New York: The New Press, 1996.

Clarke, Edward H. *Sex in Education; or, A Fair Chance for Girls.* Boston: James R. Osgood, 1874. pds.lib.harvard.edu/pds/view/2574354?n=2&s=4&image size=1200&rotation=0 (accessed October 26, 2009)

Collins, Gail. *America's Women: 400 Years of Dolls, Drudges, Helpmates, and Heroines.* New York: HarperCollins, 2003.

Cooper, Anna Julia. *A Voice from the South: By a Black Woman of the South.* Xenia, OH: The Aldine Printing House, 1892.

Cott, Nancy F. *Bonds of Womanhood: "Woman's Sphere" in New England, 1780–1835,* 2nd ed. New Haven, CT: Yale University, 1997.

Dally, Ann. *Inventing Motherhood: The Consequences of an Ideal.* New York: Schocken, 1982.

Dennett, Mary Ware. "The Sex Side of Life: An Explanation for Young People." In *"The Sex Side of Life": Mary Ware Dennet's Pioneering Battle for Birth Control and Sex Education,* by Constance M. Chen, p. 307. New York: The New Press, 1996.

Dill, Bonnie Thornton. "Our Mothers' Grief: Racial Ethnic Women and the Maintenance of Families." *Journal of Family History,* 13, no. 4 (1988): 415–431.

DuBois, Ellen Carol, and Lynn Dumenil. *Through Women's Eyes: An American History with Documents.* Boston: Bedford/St. Martin's, 2005.

Ehrenreich, Barbara, and Deirdre English. *For Her Own Good: 150 Years of the Experts' Advice to Women.* New York: Anchor, 1978.

Feldstein, Ruth. *Motherhood in Black and White: Race and Sex in American Liberalism, 1930–1965.* Ithaca, NY: Cornell University, 2000.

Freedman, Estelle B. *No Turning Back: The History of Feminism and the Future of Women.* London: Profile, 2002.

Giddings, Paula. *When and Where I Enter: The Impact of Black Women on Race and Sex in America.* New York: William Morrow, 1984, and Perennial, 2001.

Gilman, Charlotte Perkins. *Women and Economics: A Study of the Economic Relation Between Men and Women as a Factor in Social Evolution,* edited by Carl Degler. New York: Harper and Row, (1898) 1966.

Goldman, Emma. *Anarchism and Other Essays.* 1910. Dallas: Taylor, 1969.

Gordon, Linda. "Why Nineteenth-Century Feminists Did Not Support 'Birth Control' and Twentieth-Century Feminists Do: Feminism, Reproduction, and the Family." In *Rethinking the Family: Some Feminist Questions,* edited by Barrie Thorne and Marilyn Yalom, pp. 140–154. Boston: Northeastern University, 1992.

Greenspan, Karen. *The Timetables of Women's History: A Chronology of the Most Important People and Events in Women's History.* New York: Simon and Schuster, 1994.

Howe, Julia Ward. *Sex and Education: A Reply to Dr. E. H. Clarke's "Sex in Education."* Boston: Roberts Brothers, 1874. http://pds.lib.harvard.edu/pds/view/2585736?n=2&s=4 (accessed October 27, 2009)

Key, Ellen. *The Woman Movement,* translated by Mamah Bouton Borthwick. New York: Putnam, 1912.

Koven, Seth, and Sonya Michel, eds. *Mothers of a New World: Maternalist Politics and the Origins of Welfare States.* New York: Routledge, 1993.

Mann, Barbara Alice. *Iroquoian Women: The Gantowisas.* New York: Peter Lang, 2000.

Margolis, Maxine L. *True to Her Nature: Changing Advice to American Women.* Prospect Heights, IL: Waveland, 2000.

Mink, Gwendolyn. *The Wages of Motherhood: Inequality in the Welfare State, 1917–1942*. Ithaca, NY: Cornell University, 1995.

National Women's History Museum. "Motherhood, Social Service, and Political Reform: Political Culture and Imagery of American Woman Suffrage." www.nwhm .org/exhibits/toc.html (accessed November 24, 2009)

Parsons, Elsie Clews. "Feminism and the Family." *International Journal of Ethics*, 28, (1917): 52–58.

Rosenberg, Rosalind. "In Search of Woman's Nature, 1850–1920." *Feminist Studies*, 3, no. 1/2 (1975): 141–153.

Ryan, Mary P. *Womanhood in America: From Colonial Times to the Present*. New York: New Viewpoints, 1975.

Sanger, Margaret. "Letter to Supporters. October 28, 1914." In *Women's Letters: America from the Revolutionary War to the Present*, edited by Lisa Grunwald and Stephen J. Adler, pp. 466–467. New York: Dial, 2005.

Shulman, Alix Kates, ed. *Red Emma Speaks: Selected Writings and Speeches by Emma Goldman*. New York: Vintage, 1972.

Sigerman, Harriet, ed. *The Columbia Documentary History of American Women Since 1941*. New York: Columbia University, 2003.

Solinger, Rickie. *Pregnancy and Power: A Short History of Reproductive Politics in America*. New York: New York University, 2005.

Stanton, Elizabeth Cady, Susan B. Anthony, and Matilda Joslyn Gage, eds. *A History of Woman Suffrage, Vol. 1*. 1889. New York: Arno, 1969.

Stowe, Harriet Beecher. *Uncle Tom's Cabin; or, Life Among the Lowly*. Boston: John P. Jewett & Company, 1852. Available online at http://xroads.virginia.edu/~HYPER/ STOWE/stowe.html (accessed March 12, 2009).

Terrell, Mary Church. "In Union There is Strength." BlackPast.org. www.blackpast .org/?q=1897-mary-church-terrell-union-there-strength (accessed July 5, 2009)

Thurer, Shari L. *The Myths of Motherhood: How Culture Reinvents the Good Mother*. Boston: Houghton Mifflin, 1994.

U.S. Department of Labor Children's Bureau. "Infant Care," Bureau Publication No. 8. Washington DC: Government Printing Office, 1921.

Van Gelder, Lindsy. "Countdown to Motherhood: When Should You Have a Baby?" *Ms.* (December 1986): 37–41.

Wedgwood, Julia. "Male and Female Created He Them." *Contemporary Review* (July 1889): 120–133.

White, Deborah Gray. *Too Heavy a Load: Black Women in Defense of Themselves, 1894–1994*. New York: W. W. Norton, 1994.

Williams, Fannie Barrier. "The Club Movement Among Colored Women of America." In *A New Negro for a New Century: An Accurate and Up-to-Date Record of the Upward Struggles of the Negro Race*, edited by Booker T. Washington, N. B. Wood, and Fannie Barrier Williams, 1900, pp. 379–428. New York: Arno, 1969.

Wollstonecraft, Mary. *A Vindication of the Rights of Woman*. 1792. New York: Alfred A. Knopf, 1992.

Chapter 3

Beal, Frances. "Double Jeopardy: To Be Black and Female." In *The Black Woman: An Anthology,* edited by Toni Cade, pp. 90–100. New York: Signet, 1970.

Bernard, Jessie. *The Future of Motherhood.* New York: Penguin, 1974.

Black Women's Liberation Group. "Statement on Birth Control." In *Sisterhood Is Powerful: An Anthology of Writings from the Women's Liberation Movement,* edited by Robin Morgan, pp. 360–361. New York: Vintage, 1970.

Bond, Jean Carey, and Patricia Peery. "Has the Black Male Been Castrated?" *Liberator,* 9 (May 1969): 4–8.

Boston Women's Health Book Collective. *Our Bodies, Ourselves.* New York: Simon and Schuster, 1973.

Cade, Toni, ed. *The Black Woman: An Anthology.* New York: Signet, 1970.

———. "On the Issue of Roles." In *The Black Woman: An Anthology,* pp. 101–110. New York: Signet, 1970.

Chavez, Jennie V. "A New Revolution Within a Revolution Has Begun." *Mademoiselle* (April 1972): 82, 150–152. In *The Columbia Documentary History of American Women Since 1941,* edited by Harriet Sigerman, pp. 266–269. New York: Columbia University, 2003.

Chodorow, Nancy J. *The Reproduction of Mothering.* Berkeley and Los Angeles: University of California, 1978.

Comprehensive Child Development Act of 1971. ED056767—Part 3. (Joint Hearings Before the Subcommittee on Employment, Manpower, and Poverty and the Subcommittee on Children and Youth of the Committee on Labor and Public Welfare, United States Senate, Ninety-Second Congress, First Session on S.1512)

Coontz, Stephanie. *The Way We Never Were: American Families and the Nostalgia Trap.* New York: Basic, 1992.

Dally, Ann. *Inventing Motherhood: The Consequences of an Ideal.* New York: Schocken, 1982.

Davis, Angela. "Reflections on the Black Woman's Role in the Community of Slaves." *Black Scholar,* 3, no. 4 (December 1971): 2–15.

———. *Women, Race, and Class.* New York: Random House, 1981, 1984.

de Beauvoir, Simone. *The Second Sex.* New York: Alfred A. Knopf, 1952.

Dinnerstein, Dorothy. *The Mermaid and the Minotaur: Sexual Arrangements and Human Malaise.* New York: Harper Colophon, 1976.

Driscoll, Carol. "The Abortion Problem." In *Voices from Women's Liberation,* edited by Leslie B. Tanner, pp. 207–214. New York: Signet, 1970.

Feldstein, Ruth. *Motherhood in Black and White: Race and Sex in American Liberalism, 1930–1965.* Ithaca, NY: Cornell University, 2000.

Firestone, Shulamith. *The Dialectic of Sex: The Case for Feminist Revolution.* New York: Morrow Quill, 1970.

Friedan, Betty. *The Feminine Mystique.* New York: W. W. Norton, 1963.

Gordon, Linda. "Functions of the Family." In *Voices from Women's Liberation,* edited by Leslie B. Tanner, pp. 181–188. New York: Signet, 1970.

Glassman, Carol. "Women and the Welfare System." In *Sisterhood Is Powerful: An Anthology of Writings from the Women's Liberation Movement,* edited by Robin Morgan, pp. 102–115. New York: Vintage, 1970.

Global Women's Strike. "Selma James." www.globalwomenstrike.net/England/ SelmaBiography.htm (accessed November 25, 2009)

Griswold v. Connecticut. U.S. Supreme Court. 381 U.S. 479, 1965.

Gross, Louise, and Phyllis MacEwan. "On Day Care." In *Voices from Women's Liberation,* edited by Leslie B. Tanner, pp. 199–207. New York: Signet, 1970.

Hays, Sharon. *The Cultural Contradictions of Motherhood.* New Haven, CT: Yale University, 1996.

Kornbluh, Felicia Ann. *The Battle for Welfare Rights: Politics and Poverty in Modern America.* Philadelphia: University of Pennsylvania, 2007.

Lazarre, Jane. *The Mother Knot.* New York: McGraw-Hill, 1976.

Lorde, Audre. "Man Child: A Black Lesbian Feminist's Response." In *Sister Outsider: Essays and Speeches,* pp. 72–80. Berkeley, CA: The Crossing, 1984.

Margolis, Maxine L. *True to Her Nature: Changing Advice to American Women.* Prospect Heights, IL: Waveland, 2000.

May, Elaine Tyler. *Homeward Bound.* New York: Basic, 2008.

Mink, Gwendolyn. *The Wages of Motherhood: Inequality in the Welfare State, 1917–1942.* Ithaca, NY: Cornell University, 1995.

Mitchell, Juliet. *Woman's Estate.* New York: Pantheon, 1971.

Moraga, Cherríe, and Gloria Anzaldúa, eds. *This Bridge Called My Back: Writings by Radical Women of Color.* New York: Kitchen Table, 1981.

Morgan, Robin, ed. *Sisterhood Is Powerful: An Anthology of Writings from the Women's Liberation Movement.* New York: Vintage, 1970.

Moynihan, Daniel Patrick. "The Negro Family: The Case for National Action." United States Department of Labor, Office of Planning and Research, March 1965. www.dol .gov/oasam/programs/history/webid-meynihan.htm (accessed October 26, 2009)

National Organization for Women. "History of NOW." www.now.org/history (accessed March 25, 2009)

———. "Homemaker's Bill of Rights: Economic Recognition for Homemakers," 1978. www.now.org/issues/mothers/bill_of_rights.html (accessed September 9, 2009)

Our Bodies, Ourselves. www.ourbodiesourselves.org (accessed July 6, 2009)

Rich, Adrienne. *Of Woman Born: Motherhood as Experience and Institution.* New York: W. W. Norton, 1976.

Roe v. Wade. U.S. Supreme Court. 410 U.S. 113, 1973.

Sigerman, Harriet, ed. *The Columbia Documentary History of American Women Since 1941.* New York: Columbia University, 2003.

Smith, Lillian. *Killers of the Dream.* New York: W. W. Norton, 1949, 1961.

Snitow, Ann. "Feminism and Motherhood: An American Reading." In *Feminist Review,* 40, no.1 (1992): 32–51.

Spock, Benjamin. *The Common Sense Book of Baby and Child Care.* New York: Duell,

Sloan and Pearce, 1946.

Tanner, Leslie B., ed. *Voices from Women's Liberation*. New York: Signet, 1970.

Tillmon, Johnnie. "Welfare as a Women's Issue." *Ms.*, February 1972.

Umansky, Lauri. *Motherhood Reconceived: Feminism and the Legacies of the Sixties*. New York: New York University, 1996.

U.S. Department of Labor Children's Bureau. "Infant Care," Bureau Publication No. 8, rev. ed. Washington DC: Government Printing Office, 1963.

Wallace, Michele. *Black Macho and the Myth of the Super-Woman*. New York: Dial, 1978.

White, Deborah Gray. *Too Heavy a Load: Black Women in Defense of Themselves, 1894–1994*. New York: W. W. Norton, 1994.

WITCH (Women Interested in Toppling Consumption Holidays). "Mother's Day Incantation." In *Sisterhood Is Powerful: An Anthology of Writings from the Women's Liberation Movement*, edited by Robin Morgan, p. 550. New York: Vintage, 1970.

Wylie, Philip. *Generation of Vipers*. Champaign, IL: Dalkey Archive, 1942.

Chapter 4

Aldous, Joan, and Wilfried Dumon. "Family Policy in the 1980s: Controversy and Consensus." *Journal of Marriage and the Family,* 52 (1990): 1136–1151.

Allen, Jeffner. *Lesbian Philosophy: Explorations*. Palo Alto, CA: Institute of Lesbian Studies, 1986.

Bell-Scott, Patricia, Beverly Guy-Sheftall, Jacqueline Jones Royster, Janet Sims-Wood, et al., eds. *Double Stitch: Black Women Write About Mothers and Daughters*. Boston: Beacon, 1991.

Bean, Kellie. *Post-Backlash Feminism: Women and the Media Since Reagan-Bush*. London: McFarland, 2007.

Berry, Cecelie S. *Rise Up Singing: Black Women Writers on Motherhood*. New York: Harlem Moon, 2004.

Black Women's Health Imperative. www.blackwomenshealth.org (accessed May 16, 2009)

Bolotin, Susan. "Voices of the Post-Feminist Generation." *New York Times Magazine* (October 17, 1982). www.lexisnexis.com/us/lnacademic/auth/checkbrowser.do?ipco unter=1&cookieState=0&rand=0.353582980169618&bhcp=1

Chase, Susan E., and Mary F. Rogers. *Mothers and Children: Feminist Analyses and Personal Narratives*. New Brunswick, NJ: Rutgers University, 2001.

The Clearinghouse on International Developments in Child, Youth and Family Policies at Columbia University. "United States, Country Summary." www.childpolicyintl .org/countries/us01.htm (accessed April 30, 2009)

Coontz, Stephanie. *The Way We Never Were: American Families and the Nostalgia Trap*. New York: Basic, 1992.

Copper, Baba. "The Radical Potential in Lesbian Mothering of Daughters." In *Politics of the Heart: A Lesbian Parenting Anthology,* edited by Sandra Pollack and Jeanne Vaughn, pp. 233–240. Ann Arbor, MI: Firebrand, 1987.

Correll, Shelly J., Stephen Benard, and In Paik. "Getting a Job: Is There a Motherhood Penalty?" *American Journal of Sociology*, 112, no. 5 (March 2007): 1297–1338.

Davis, Angela Y. *Women, Culture, and Politics*. New York: Random House/Vintage, 1984, 1989.

Douglas, Susan J., and Meredith W. Michaels. *The Mommy Myth: The Idealization of Motherhood and How It Has Undermined All Women*. New York: The Free Press, 2004.

Ehrenreich, Barbara, and Arlie Russell Hochschild. *Global Woman: Nannies, Maids, and Sex Workers in the New Economy*. New York: Metropolitan/Owl, 2002.

Faludi, Susan. *Backlash: The Undeclared War Against American Women*. New York: Doubleday, 1991.

Friedan, Betty. *The Second Stage*. New York: Summit, 1981.

Gerson, Kathleen. *Hard Choices: How Women Decide About Work, Career, and Motherhood*. Berkeley and London: University of California Press, 1985.

Glenn, Evelyn Nakano, Grace Chang, and Linda Rennie Forcey, eds. *Mothering: Ideology, Experience, and Agency*. New York: Routledge, 1994.

Gore, Ariel. *The Mother Trip: Hip Mama's Guide to Staying Sane in the Chaos of Motherhood*. Seattle: Seal, 2000.

Hays, Sharon. *The Cultural Contradictions of Motherhood*. New Haven, CT: Yale University, 1998.

Hochschild, Arlie Russell, and Anne Machung. *The Second Shift*. New York: Penguin, 1989, 2003.

hooks, bell. "Homeplace: A Site of Resistance." In *Yearning, Race, Gender, and Cultural Politics*, pp. 46–47. Cambridge, MA: South End, 1990.

Jetter, Alexis, Annelise Orleck, and Diana Taylor. *The Politics of Motherhood: Activist Voices from Left to Right*. Hanover, NH: University Press of New England, 1997.

Kantrowitz, Barbara. "Three's a Crowd." *Newsweek*, (September 1, 1986): 68–76.

Kinser, Amber E., ed. *Mothering in the Third Wave*. Toronto: Demeter, 2008.

Kinser, Amber E. "Mothering Feminist Daughters in 'Postfeminist' Times." *Journal of the Association for Research on Mothering*, 10, no. 2 (2008): 20-36.

Lewin, Ellen. "Negotiating Lesbian Motherhood: The Dialectics of Resistance and Accommodation." In *Mothering: Ideology, Experience, and Agency*, edited by Evelyn Nakano Glenn, Grace Chang, and Linda Rennie Forcey, pp. 333–350. New York: Routledge, 1994.

Mainardi, Pat. "The Politics of Housework." In *Sisterhood Is Powerful: An Anthology of Writings from the Women's Liberation Movement*, edited by Robin Morgan, pp. 447–453. New York: Vintage, 1970.

Mascha, Kristin. *This Is Not How I Thought It Would Be: Remodeling Motherhood to Get the Lives We Want Today*. New York: Berkeley, 2009.

Maushart, Susan. *The Mask of Motherhood: How Becoming a Mother Changes Everything and Why We Pretend It Doesn't*. New York: Penguin, 1999.

Mothers Ought to Have Equal Rights. www.mothersoughttohaveequalrights.org (accessed May 15, 2009)

"1963 Baptist Faith and Message Statement with 1998 Amendment." Southern Baptist Convention. www.sbc.net/bfm/bfmcomparison.asp (accessed November 27, 2009)

O'Reilly, Andrea. *Rocking the Cradle: Thoughts on Motherhood, Feminism, and the Possibilty of Empowered Mothering*, p. 30. Toronto: Demeter, 2006.

———, ed. *Maternal Theory: Essential Readings*. Toronto: Demeter, 2007.

Peri, Camille, and Kate Moses, eds. *Mothers Who Think*. New York: Washington Square/ Salon, 1999.

Peskowitz, Miriam. *The Truth Behind the Mommy Wars: Who Decides What Makes a Good Mother?* Emeryville, CA: Seal, 2005.

Polikoff, Nancy. "Lesbian Choosing Children: The Personal Is Political Revisited." 1987. Reprinted in *Maternal Theory: Essential Readings*, edited by Andrea O'Reilly, pp. 194–200. Toronto: Demeter, 2007.

Pollack, Sandra, and Jeanne Vaughn, eds. *Politics of the Heart: A Lesbian Parenting Anthology.* Ann Arbor, MI: Firebrand, 1987.

Quayle, Dan. Address to the Commonwealth Club of California (On Family Values). May 19, 1992. www.vicepresidentdanquayle.com/speeches_StandingFirm_CCC_ 1.html (accessed November 24, 2009)

Rothman, Barbara Katz. *Weaving a Family: Untangling Race and Adoption.* Boston: Beacon, 2005.

Ruddick, Sara. "Maternal Thinking." *Feminist Studies,* 6, no. 2 (Summer 1980): 342–367.

———. "Preservative Love and Military Destruction: Some Reflections on Mothering and Peace." In *Mothering: Essays in Feminist Theory*, edited by Joyce Trebilcot, pp. 231–262. Savage, MD: Rowman and Littlefield, 1983.

Ryan, Maura. "An Open Letter to the Lesbians Who Have Mothered Before Me." In *Mothering in the Third Wave*, edited by Amber E. Kinser, pp. 31–37. Toronto: Demeter, 2008.

Sigerman, Harriet, ed. *The Columbia Documentary History of American Women Since 1941.* New York: Columbia University, 2003.

Silliman, Jael, Marlene Fried, Loretta Ross, and Elena R. Gutiérez. *Undivided Rights: Women of Color Organize for Reproductive Justice.* Cambridge, MA: South End, 2004.

Snitow, Ann. "Feminism and Motherhood: An American Reading." *Feminist Review,* 40, no.1 (1992): 32–51.

Solinger, Rickie. *Pregnancy and Power: A Short History of Reproductive Politics in America.* New York: New York University, 2005.

Tobias, Sheila. *Faces of Feminism: An Activist's Reflections on the Women's Movement.* Boulder, CO: Westview, 1997.

Trebilcot, Joyce, ed. *Mothering: Essays in Feminist Theory.* Savage, MD: Rowman and Littlefield, 1983.

Trenka, Jane Jeong, Julia Chinyere Oparah, and Sun Yung Shin, eds. *Outsiders Within: Writing on Transracial Adoption.* Cambridge, MA: South End, 2006.

Umansky, Lauri. *Motherhood Reconceived: Feminism and the Legacies of the Sixties.* New York: New York University, 1996.

Warner, Judith. *Perfect Madness: Motherhood in the Age of Anxiety.* New York: Riverhead, 2005.

Weideger, Paula. "Womb Worship." *Ms.* (February 1988): 54–57.

White House Working Group on the Family. "The Family: Preserving America's Future." Washington, DC: Domestic Policy Council, 1986. Available at www.eric.ed.gov/ERICDocs/data/ericdocs2sql/content_storage_01/0000019b/80/20/03/b8.pdf (accessed May 17, 2009).

Williams, Joan C., Jessica Manvell, and Stephanie Bronstein. "Opt Out or Pushed Out? How the Press Covers Work/Family Conflict: The Untold Story of Why Women Leave the Workforce." The Center for WorkLife Law, University of California Hastings College of the Law, 2006. www.uchastings.edu/site_files/WLL/OptOutPushedOut.pdf (accessed March 14, 2009)

Women of All Red Nations. "Radiation: Dangerous to Pine Ridge Women." In *Akwesasne Notes,* vol. 12, no. 1 (1980).

Chapter 5

Association for Research on Mothering. www.yorku.ca/arm (accessed March 28, 2009)

Baumgardner, Jennifer, and Amy Richards. *Grassroots: A Field Guide for Feminist Activism.* New York: Farrar, Straus and Giroux, 2005.

Black Moms Club. blackmomsclub.ning.com (accessed April 1, 2009)

Blades, Joan, and Kristen Rowe-Finkbeiner. *The Motherhood Manifesto: What America's Moms Want—And What to Do About It.* New York: Nation, 2006.

Brain, Child. www.brainchildmag.com (accessed May 22, 2009)

Buchanan, Andrea J., and Amy Hudock. *Literary Mama: Reading for the Maternally Inclined.* Emeryville, CA: Seal, 2006.

Children's Defense Fund. www.childrensdefense.org/helping-americas-children/cradle-to-prison-pipeline-campaign (accessed October 27, 2009)

Choice Moms. www.choicemoms.org (accessed April 1, 2009)

Colorado Organization for Latina Opportunity and Reproductive Rights, www.colorlatina.org (accessed May 22, 2009)

Crittenden, Ann. *The Price of Motherhood: Why the Most Important Job in the World Is Still the Least Valued.* New York: Henry Holt, 2002.

DiQuinzio, Patrice. "The Politics of the Mother's Movement in the United States: Possibilities and Pitfalls." *Journal of the Association for Research in Mothering,* 8, nos. 1/2. (Winter/Summer 2006): 55–71.

EcoMom. http://ecomom.com (accessed October 26, 2009)

Family Equality Council. www.familyequality.org (accessed April 15, 2009)

Flavin, Jeanne. *Our Bodies, Our Crimes: The Policing of Women's Reproduction in America.* New York: New York University, 2008.

Friedman, May. "It Takes a (Virtual) Village: Mothering on the Internet." In *Motherhood at the 21st Century: Experience, Identity, Policy, Agency,* edited by Andrea O'Reilly. New York: Columbia University, 2010.

Girl-Mom. www.girlmom.com (accessed May 22, 2009)

Global Action for Children. www.globalactionforchildren.org (accessed May 16, 2009)

Hewett, Heather. Talkin' 'Bout a Revolution: Building a Mothers' Movement in the Third Wave. *Journal of the Association for Research on Mothering*, 8, nos. 1/2 (Winter/Summer 2006): 34–54.

Hip Mama. www.hipmama.com (accessed March 25, 2009)

Holistic Moms Network. www.holisticmoms.org (accessed March 29, 2009)

INCITE! Women of Color Against Violence. *Color of Violence: The INCITE! Anthology*. Cambridge, MA: South End, 2006.

———. *The Revolution Will Not Be Funded: Beyond the Nonprofit Industrial Complex*. Cambridge, MA: South End, 2007.

INCITE! www.incite-national.org (accessed May 22, 2009)

International Mothers Network. www.internationalmothersnetwork.org/home.html (accessed April 1, 2009)

Literary Mama. www.literarymama.com (accessed May 22, 2009)

Mamapalooza. www.mamapalooza.com/home.html (accessed March 26, 2009)

Mamaphonic. www.mamaphonic.com (accessed May 22, 2009)

Mamazine. www.mamazine.com (accessed May 22, 2009)

Maybe Baby. www.maybebabyseattle.org/Maybe_Baby_Seattle/Home.html (accessed April 17, 2009)

Mocha Moms. www.mochamoms.org (accessed March 26, 2009)

Mombian. www.mombian.com (accessed April 15, 2009)

MOMbo. www.mombo.org (accessed October 26, 2009)

Mommy Too! mommytoomag.com (accessed March 28, 2009)

MomsRising. www.momsrising.org (accessed March 28, 2009)

Mom Writers Literary Magazine. www.momwriterslitmag.com (accessed May 22, 2009)

Mothers Acting Up. www.mothersactingup.org (accessed May 22, 2009)

Mothers and More. www.mothersandmore.org (accessed March 28, 2009)

Mothers Are Women. www.mothersarewomen.com (accessed May 22, 2009)

Mothers in Charge. www.mothersincharge.org (accessed May 22, 2009)

Mothers Movement Online. www.mothersmovement.org (accessed March 26, 2009)

Mothers on the Move/Madres en Movimiento. www.mothersonthemove.org (accessed May 22, 2009)

Mothers Ought to Have Equal Rights. www.mothersoughttohaveequalrights.org (accessed March 28, 2009)

Mothers Who Think. dir.salon.com/topics/mwt (accessed May 22, 2009)

Museum of Motherhood. www.museumofmotherhood.org/Info.html (accessed May 22, 2009)

National Advocates for Pregnant Women. www.advocatesforpregnantwomen.org (accessed March 28, 2009)

National Association of Mothers' Centers. www.motherscenter.org (accessed March 26, 2009)

National Council of Women's Organizations. *50 Ways to Improve Women's Lives: The*

Essential Women's Guide for Achieving Equality, Health, and Success. San Francisco: Inner Ocean, 2005.

National Latina Institute for Reproductive Health. www.latinainstitute.org (accessed May 22, 2009)

National Organization of Single Mothers. www.singlemothers.org (accessed October 26, 2009)

Organic Green Mommy. www.organicgreenmommy.com (accessed October 26, 2009)

Silliman, Jael, Marlene Fried, Loretta Ross, and Elena R. Guitiérrez. *Undivided Rights: Women of Color Organize for Reproductive Justice.* Cambridge, MA: South End, 2004.

Single Mom. www.singlemom.com (accessed October 26, 2009)

Single Mommyhood. www.singlemommyhood.com (accessed October 26, 2009)

Single Pregnancy. www.singlepregnancy.com (accessed April 2, 2009)

SisterSong. www.sistersong.net (accessed March 29, 2009)

The Motherhood Foundation. www.museumofmotherhood.org/Info.html (accessed May 22, 2009)

The Motherhood Project. www.motherhoodproject.org (accessed March 29, 2009)

The Rainbow Babies. www.therainbowbabies.com (accessed April 15, 2009)

The Young Mommies Homesite. www.youngmommies.com (accessed October 26, 2009)

TransParentcy. www.transparentcy.org (accessed April 1, 2009)

Tucker, Judith Stadtman. "Mothering in the Digital Age." In *Mothering in the Third Wave,* edited by Amber E. Kinser, pp. 199–212. Toronto: Demeter, 2008.

United Mothers Opposing Violence Everywhere. Torontopedia. www.torontopedia.ca/United_Mothers_Opposing_Violence_Everywhere (accessed March 29, 2009)

Welfare Warriors. www.welfarewarriors.org (accessed March 29, 2009)

INDEX

birth control. *See* contraception

birthing: 5, 57

bitterness: 14

Black Feminist Thought (Collins): 15

Black Macho and the Myth of the Super-Woman (Wallace): 78

Black Moms Club: 144

The Black Woman (Cade, ed.): 79

black women. *See* women of color

black-women's clubs: 46–49, 62

Black Women's Health Imperative: 116

Black Women's Liberation Group (BWLG): 91

Blades, Joan: 155

blogging: 5, 130, 131

bodies, women's: breaking silence around 60; CR groups on 89; education as harming reproductivity of 36–38; *Our Bodies, Ourselves* 89–90; Victorian perception of 56

Bolden, Dorothy: 73

Bolotin, Susan: 116

Bond, Jean Carey: 75

bonobo chimpanzees: 20

Boston Women's Health Book Collective: 89, 90

Brain, Child: 149

breast milk contaminants: 101

Brown, Murphy: 118–119

Brundage, Joanne: 154

Burwell, Dollie: 100

C

Cade, Toni: 79, 91

Calixte, Shana: 5

Campaign for a Commercial-Free Childhood: 134

care: caregivers 20; coalitions among caregivers 160; compensation for 153; as done by mothers 84; gender dualism in 10; by immigrant workers 128–129; of infants 53; maternal knowledge as arising from 19–20; of men 46; varying assumptions on 17; of women and the

earth 6–7; *see also* childrearing

Catt, Carrie Chapman: 42

change: 162–163

Chavez, Jennie: 91–94

childcare: institutionalized 55; Nixon on 80; restructuring 112; social acceptance of 119–120

Child Development Act (1971): 80

childrearing: Benjamin Spock on 65; by bitter, frustrated women 14; changing mores of 70–71; communal 4, 34, 47, 64; compensation for 153; division of labor within 112; employment as compromising 33; by entire family 28, 72; middle-class ideas of 52–53; as non-instinctual 19; women as educators on 5

children: assumptions on the nature of 16, 17; decision to have viii, ix; effects of employment on 123; gender socialization of 84; grown-up, poorly "adjusted" 63–64; lesbians raising male 85–86; life without 90, 97, 111; maternal feelings toward 19; "needs" of 22; parents as blamed for 102; as raised for consumption 65; sacrilizing 120; social acceptance of daycare for 119–120; social activism for 135–137; as "tabula rasa" 29; Terrell on 50–51; welfare for 52

Children's Bureau: 52–54, 62, 71

Children's Defense Fund: 136

Chisholm, Shirley: 72

Chodorow, Nancy: 84

Choice Moms: 147

Civil Rights Act: 72

civil rights movement: 68–69

Civil War, women's response to: 12–13

Clarke, Dr. Edward H.: 36

class issues: in communal childrearing 47; difference 22–23; employment vs. motherhood 33; poverty as blamed on the poor 102; social activism on 73; *see also* working-class/poor women

Clinton, Bill: 119

ACKNOWLEDGMENTS

I WANT TO THANK MY EDITOR JENNIE GOODE for her careful reads and willingness to hear me. Her knowledge of feminism and her ability to see each page as part of the larger whole turned the work into a coherent manuscript. Thanks to Brooke Warner for approaching me at the NWSA conference about my work and for keeping me in mind until the right project came along. Thanks also to copyeditor Karen Bleske for her meticulous read of the manuscript, and in particular for ensuring my sources were accurate. Thanks to the many students and staff members who helped me at various stages with research, typing, and trips to the library: Ash-Lee Henderson, Mithra Alavi, Lori Baker, Michelle Rogers, Devon Baker, Cassidy Barnes, Laketta Bingham, Frances Newman, Julie Blevins, Kelley Hatch, Anita Shell, Allison Morris, Christine Ketelaar, and K. C. Gott. Many thanks to Stephanie Langley-Earhart, who came in later as a research assistant but jumped in with both feet, turned work around speedy quick, and made critical contributions to the last chapter. Thanks to Pat Buck for help on material about the 19th century and to Stephanie Sellers for help on Native American Motherhood. I am indebted to the ETSU Research Development Committee for grant support in 2009. Thanks to my friend and colleague and major motivating force, Kelly Dorgan, for helping me laugh my way through low points, always. Thank you to my mother, Gail Walters, who laid the foundation for so much of what I'm able to do and for always making me feel wholly loved.

The people who gave the most to this project are my own family.

My children, Chelsea and Isaac, gave up lots of time with their mother so I could write about other mothers. I suspect the irony was not lost on them. Thank you for handling my brief but frequent lessons on maternal history and feminist activism with tender patience and good humor. I have loved mothering you, and that has fed me and my writing. Thank you to my partner, Patrick Cronin, for being ever willing to share our time "alone" together with my laptop and bags of books; he is the person I practiced my ideas with regularly as we rode to school. He continues to boast about this book and his feminist author-partner to anyone who will listen.

ABOUT THE AUTHOR

Amber E. Kinser, PhD, is editor of
Mothering in the Third Wave (Demeter,
2008). She earned her doctorate at
Purdue University in Communication,
with an emphasis in family and gender
studies. Her writing on feminism
and mothering has appeared in the
Journal for the Association for Research
on Mothering; Feminist Mothering, edited by Andrea O'Reilly (SUNY,
2007); *Mother Knows Best: Talking Back to the Baby Experts,* edited by
Jessica Nathanson and Laura Tuley; and the forthcoming *Encyclopedia
of Mothering* (Sage) and *Being and Thinking as an Academic Mother*
by Andrea O'Reilly and Lynn O'Brien Hallstein (Demeter). Her
work on third wave feminism (*National Women's Studies Association
Journal*) has been widely cited. Her speaking engagements focus on
gendered communication or on mothering. Formerly director of
Women's Studies, she is now professor and chair of the Department of
Communication at East Tennessee State University. She teaches in both
Women's Studies and Communication. She is the mother of a daughter
and a son. To read more about her work, visit www.amberkinser.com.

CREDITS

Chapter 1

Excerpt from Myriam Miedzian and Alisa Malinovich, *Generations: A Century of Women Speak About Their Lives* (Grove/Atlantic, 1997), is reprinted courtesy of the author. Miedzian is also the author of *Boys Will Be Boys: Breaking the Link Between Masculinity and Violence* (Doubleday, 1991; Lantern, 2002).

Chapter 2

"Just Like Joan of Arc" image originally appeared in *Puck* in 1915 and was provided by the Library of Congress.

John B. Watson photograph was provided by Johns Hopkins University.

Phyllis Wheatley Club photograph was provided by the Library of Congress, Nannie Helen Burroughs Collection.

"The Dirty Pool of Politics" postcard was reprinted by permission of the Smithsonian Institution.

"Letter to Supporters" excerpted from Margaret Sanger's 1914 pamphlet "Family Limitation." Reprinted by permission of Alex Sanger.

Chapter 3

"1950s Family Sitting at Kitchen Table Having Breakfast" photograph was provided by Corbis. © H. Armstrong Roberts/ClassicStock/Corbis.

"Beulah Sanders Gesturing at Podium" photograph was provided by Corbis. © Bettmann/Corbis.

"Women's Rights Defenders Celebrating" photograph was provided by Corbis. ©
Bettmann/Corbis.

"Welfare as a Women's Issue," by Johnnie Tillmon, originally appeared in the first issue
of *Ms.* magazine, 1972.

"Mother's Day Incantation" excerpted with permission from Mother's Day Incantation
by WITCH (Women Interested in Toppling Consumption Holidays), in *Sisterhood Is
Powerful* (NY: Vintage, 1970), compiled, edited, and introduced by Robin Morgan. ©
1970 by Robin Morgan.

"Homemaker's Bill of Rights" was reprinted with the permission of the National
Organization for Women. This is a historical document and may not reflect the current
language or priorities of the organization.

Chapter 4
"Reagan and the Three Sycophants" cartoon reprinted by permission of Paul D.
Candelaria.

"Woman's Work" cartoon reprinted by permission of msnbc.com. © 2009, Duane
Hoffman.

Mother and child cartoon used with the permission of Steve Kelley and Creators
Syndicate. All rights reserved.

"An Open Letter to the Lesbians Who Have Mothered Before Me" from *Mothering
in the Third Wave* by Amber E. Kinser is reprinted by permission of Association for
Research on Mothering and Demeter Press.

"The Motherhood Religion" from *Perfect Madness: Motherhood in the Age of Anxiety*
by Judith Warner, copyright © 2005 by Judith Warner. Used with permission of
Riverhead Books, an imprint of Penguin Group (USA) Inc.

Chapter 5
Mothers on the Move photograph is reprinted by permission of *New York's Daily News*
© *Daily News LP.*

Alyson Palmer image is reprinted by permission of Mamapalooza and Alyson Palmer.
Photograph by Elizabeth Ziff. © Alyson Palmer, 2005.

Family Equality Council portrait reprinted by permission of Amber Davis Tourlentes.

SELECTED TITLES FROM SEAL PRESS

For more than thirty years, Seal Press has published groundbreaking books. By women. For women. Visit our website at www.sealpress.com and our blog at www.sealpress.com/blog.

The Maternal Is Political: Women Writers at the Intersection of Motherhood and Social Change, edited by Shari MacDonald Strong. $15.95, 978-1-58005-243-6. Exploring the vital connection between motherhood and social change, *The Maternal Is Political* features thirty powerful literary essays by women striving to make the world a better place for children and families—both their own and other women's.

The Truth Behind the Mommy Wars: Who Decides What Makes a Good Mother?, by Miriam Peskowitz. $15.95, 978-1-58005-129-3. A groundbreaking book that reveals the truth behind the "wars" between working mothers and stay-at-home moms.

Women of Color and Feminism: Seal Studies, by Maythee Rojas. $14.95, 978-1-58005-272-6. Author and professor Maythee Rojas examines the intricate crossroads of being a woman of color, exploring a new discourse of feminism within ethnic studies.

Colonize This!: Young Women of Color on Today's Feminism, edited by Daisy Hernandez and Bushra Rehman. $16.95, 978-1-58005-067-8. An insight into a new generation of brilliant, outspoken women of color—how they are speaking to the concerns of a new feminism, and their place in it.

Listen Up: Voices from the Next Feminist Generation, edited by Barbara Findlen. $16.95, 978-1-58005-054-8. A collection of essays featuring the voices of today's young feminists on racism, sexuality, identity, AIDS, revolution, abortion, and much more.

Girls' Studies: Seal Studies, by Elline Lipkin. $14.95, 978-1-58005-248-1. A look at the socialization of girls in today's society and the media's influence on gender norms, expectations, and body image.